A-Z NEW...

CONTEN...

REFERENCE

Motorway	**M4**	Church or Chapel	†
A Road	**A34**	Cycleway (selected)	⚲ ....
B Road	**B4494**	Fire Station	■
		Hospital	Ⓗ
Dual Carriageway		House Numbers (A & B Roads only)	298 77
One-way Street Traffic flow on A roads is also indicated by a heavy line on the driver's left.	→ →	Information Centre	🇮
Road Under Construction Opening dates correct at time of publication.		National Grid Reference	450
Proposed Road		Police Station	▲
Restricted Access		Post Office	★
Pedestrianized Road		Safety Camera with Speed Limit Fixed cameras and long term road works cameras. Symbols do not indicate camera direction.	㉚
Track & Footpath		Toilet:	
Residential Walkway	....	without facilities for the Disabled	▽
Railway	Level Crossing Station	with facilities for the Disabled	▽
		Educational Establishment	▧
Built-up Area	OAK DR	Hospital or Healthcare Building	▢
Local Authority Boundary	— ▪ — ▪ —	Industrial Building	▦
Posttown Boundary		Leisure or Recreational Facility	▧
Postcode Boundary (within Posttown)	— — — —	Place of Interest	▢
		Public Building	▨
Map Continuation	16	Shopping Centre or Market	▧
Car Park (selected)	℗	Other Selected Buildings	▢

SCALE   1:15,840   4 inches (10.16 cm) to 1 mile,   6.31 cm to 1 kilometre

0	¼	½	¾	1 Mile

0	250	500	750	1 Kilometre

Copyright of Geographers' A-Z Map Company Limited

Fairfield Road, Borough Green, Sevenoaks, Kent TN15 8PP
Telephone: 01732 781000 (Enquiries & Trade Sales)
01732 783422 (Retail Sales)
www.az.co.uk

 Ordnance Survey®

This product includes mapping data licensed from Ordnance Survey® with the permission of the Controller of Her Majesty's Stationery Office.

© Crown Copyright 2011. All rights reserved. Licence number 100017302

Copyright © Geographers' A-Z Map Co. Ltd.

Edition 5 2012

Safety camera information supplied by www.PocketGPSWorld.com
Speed Camera Location Database Copyright 2011 © PocketGPSWorld.com

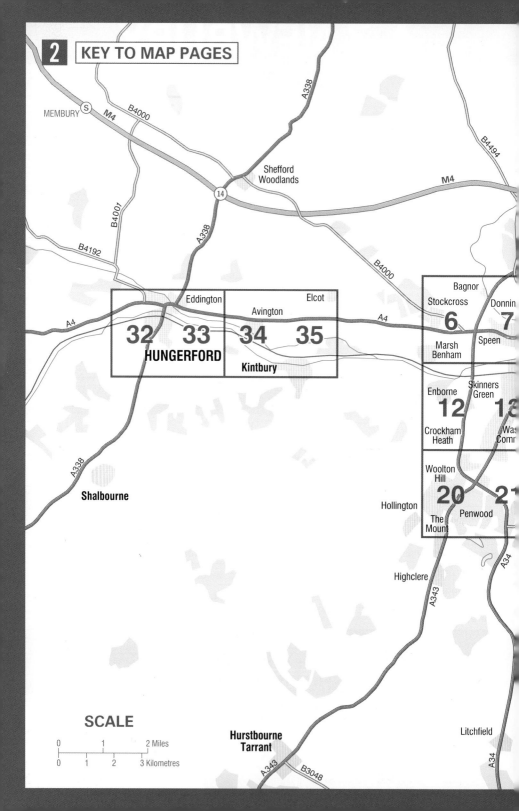

MEMBURY (S)

M4

B4000

Shefford
Woodlands

14

M4

B4494

B4001

A338

A338

B4192

B4000

B4494

Bagnor

Stockcross

Donnin

Eddington

Elcot

Avington

Speen

A4

32 33 34 35

6 7

HUNGERFORD

Marsh
Benham

Kintbury

Enborne

Skinners
Green

A338

12 13

Crockham
Heath

Was
Comr

Shalbourne

Woolton
Hill

Hollington

20 21

Penwood

The
Mount

A34

Highclere

A343

A34

SCALE

0 — 1 — 2 Miles
0 — 1 — 2 — 3 Kilometres

Hurstbourne
Tarrant

Litchfield

A343

B3048

A34

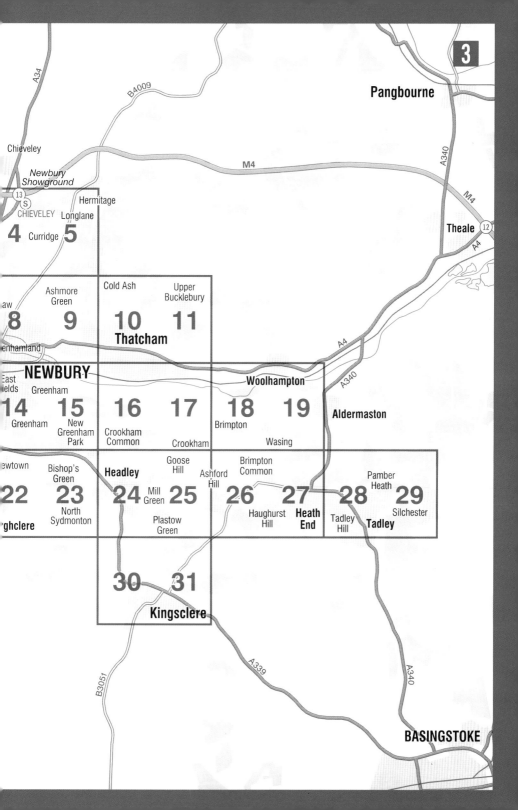

3

Pangbourne

A34

B4009

M4

A340

M4

Chieveley

Newbury Showground

13
S
CHIEVELEY   Longlane   Hermitage

4   Curridge   **5**

Theale

12

A4

A340

A4

8   Ashmore Green   Cold Ash   Upper Bucklebury

aw   **9**   **10**   **11**

enhamland   **Thatcham**

NEWBURY   Woolhampton

East ields   Greenham

14   **15**   **16**   **17**   **18**   **19**   **Aldermaston**

Greenham   New Greenham Park   Crookham Common   Crookham   Brimpton   Wasing

ewtown   Bishop's Green   **Headley**   Goose Hill   Brimpton Common   Pamber Heath

22   **23**   **24**   Mill Green   **25**   Ashford Hill   **26**   **27**   **28**   **29**

ghclere   North Sydmonton   Plastow Green   Haughurst Hill   **Heath End**   Tadley Hill   **Tadley**   Silchester

30   **31**

Kingsclere

B3051   A339   A340

BASINGSTOKE

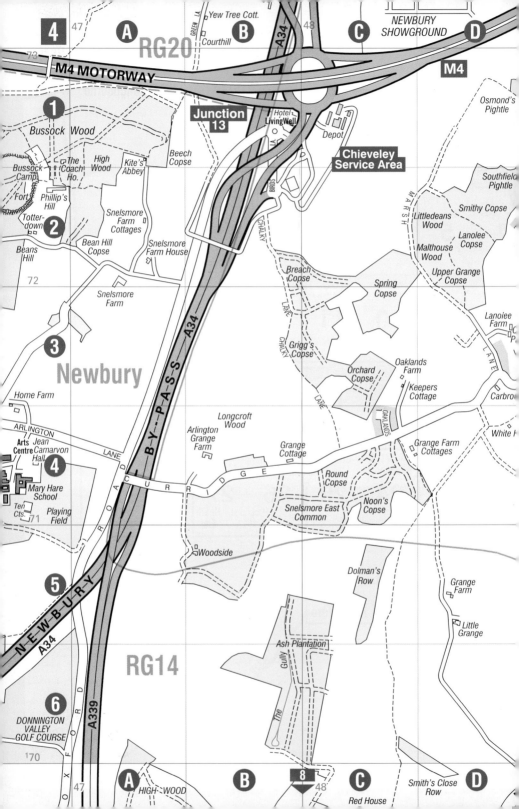

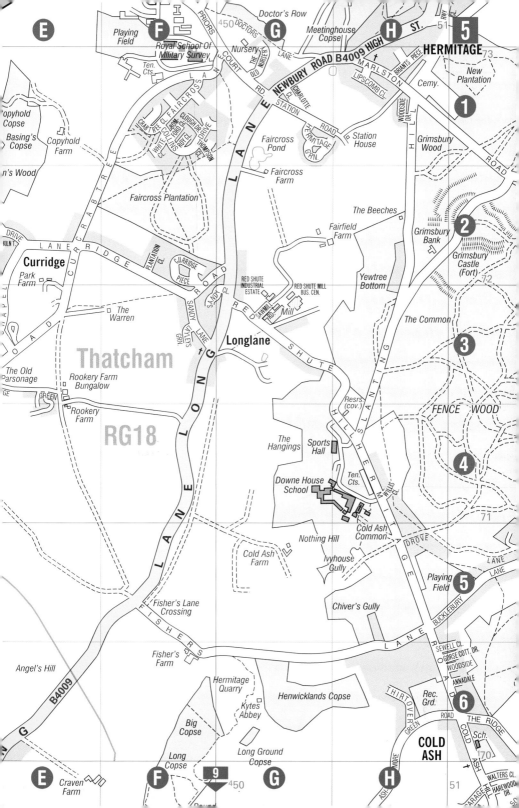

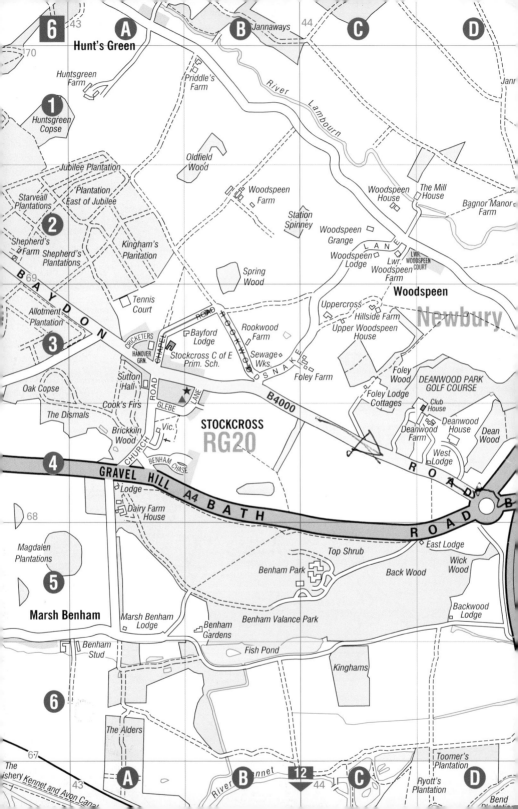

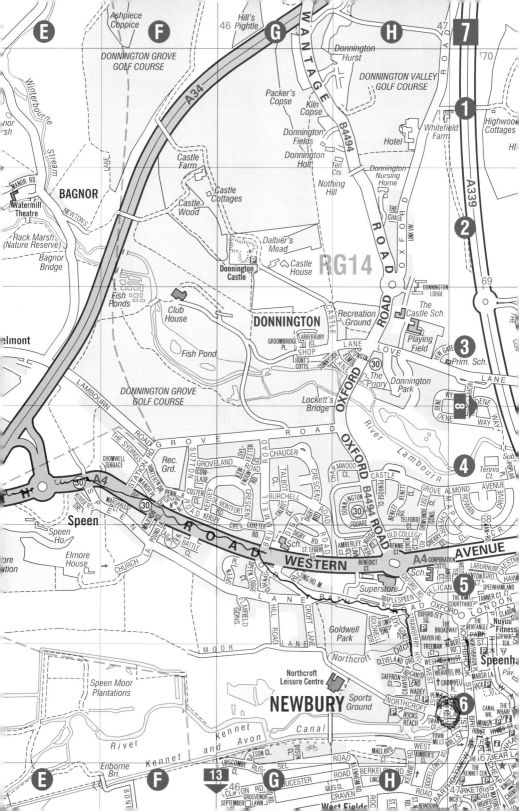

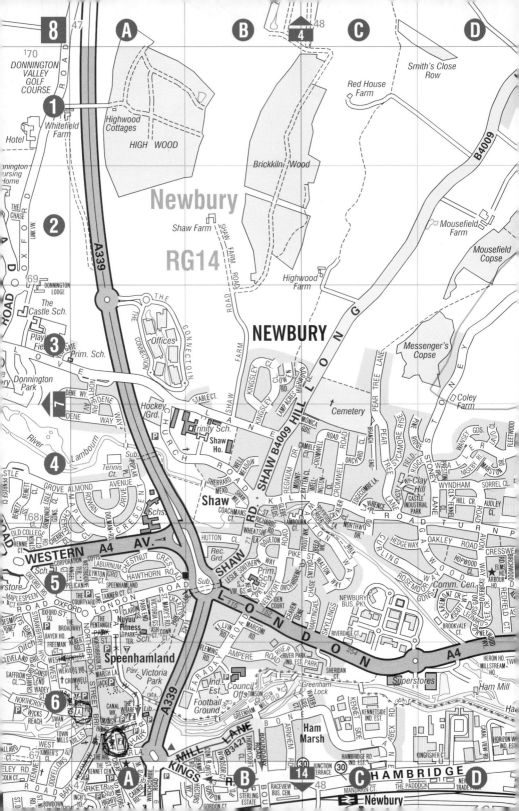

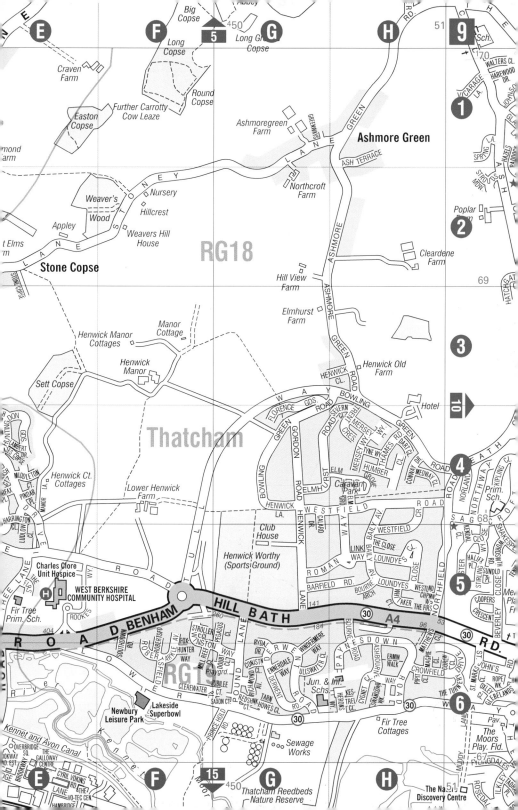

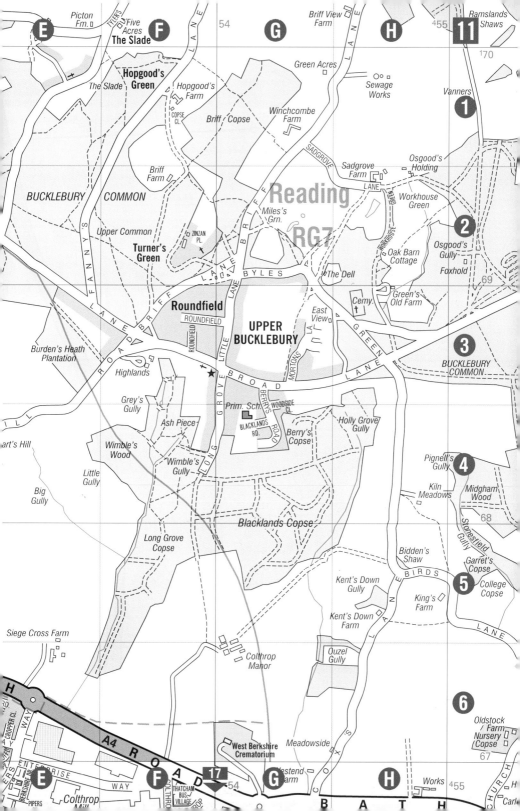

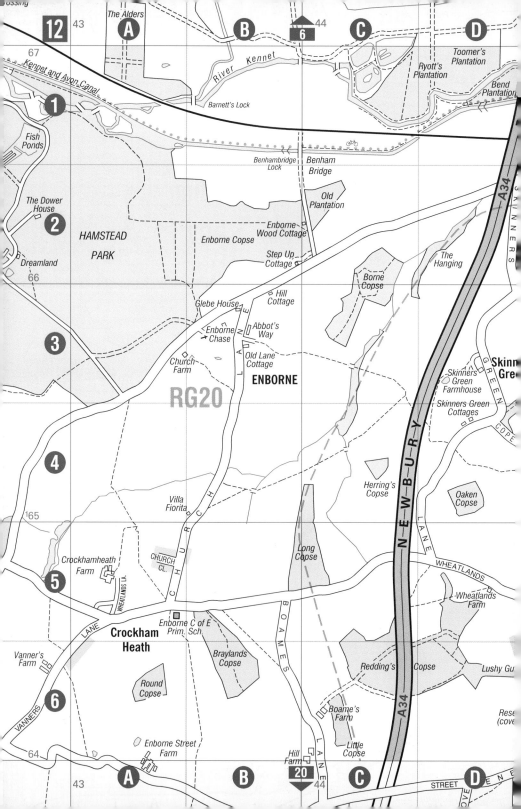

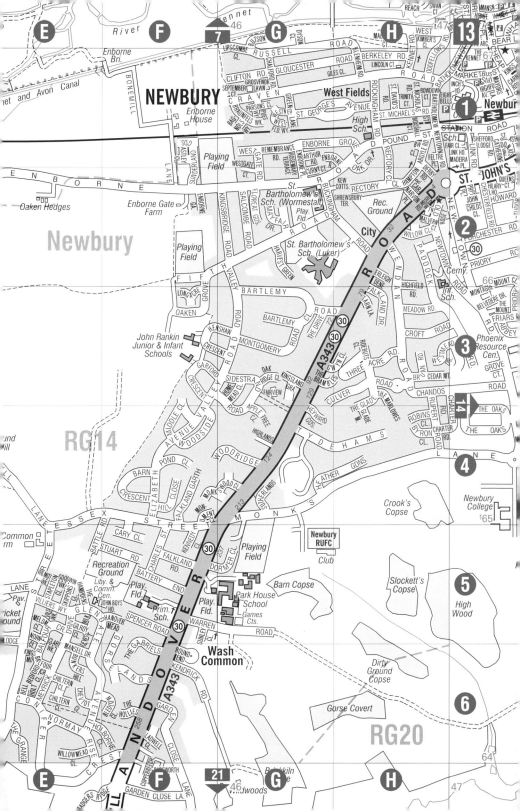

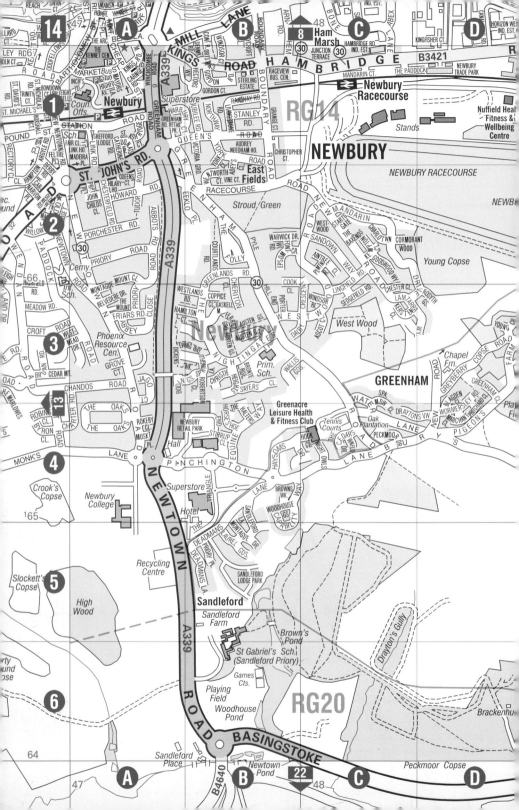

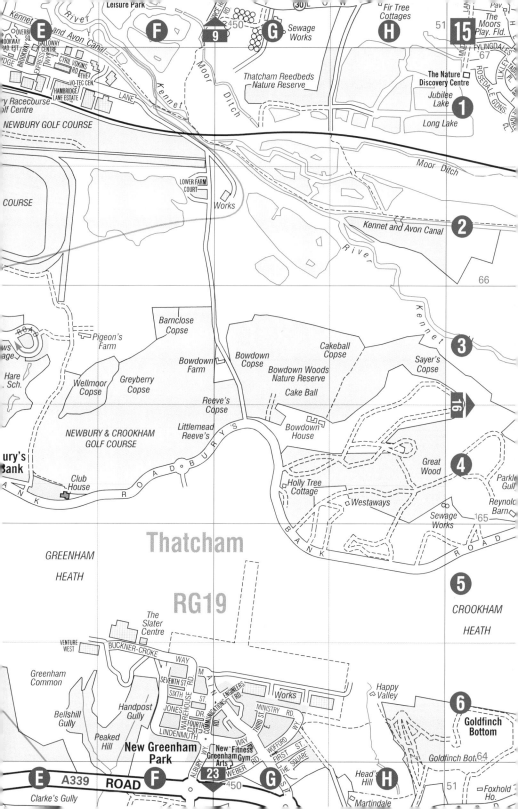

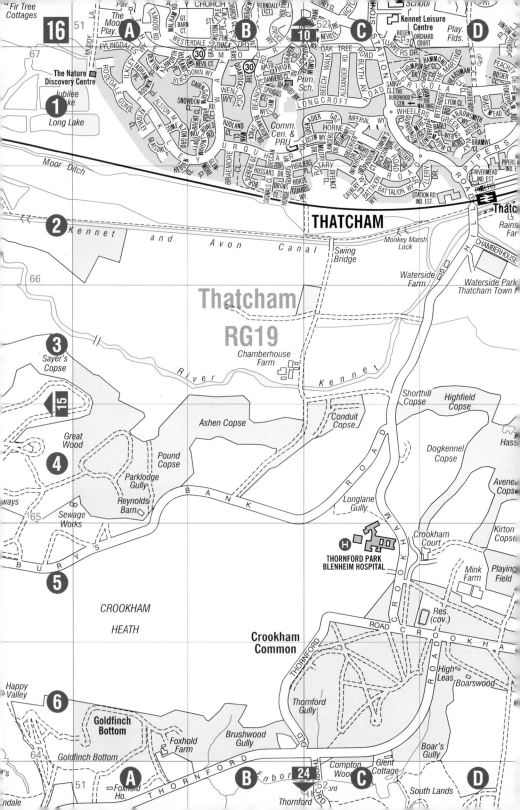

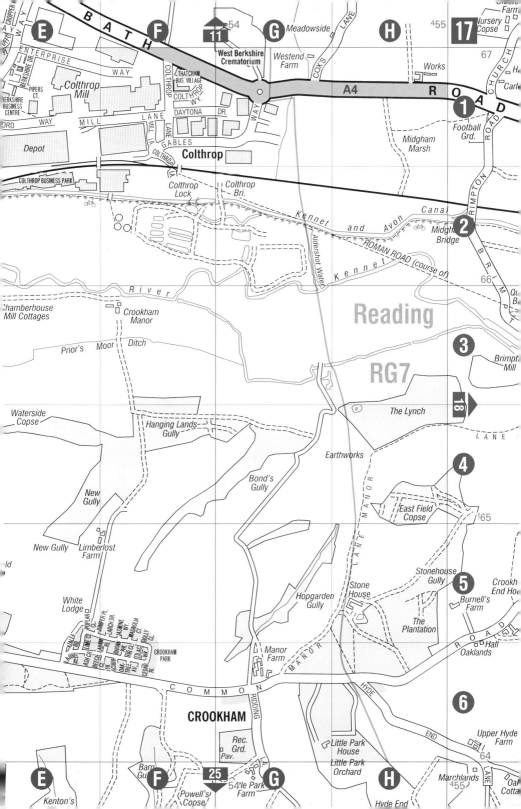

E   **F**   **G**   **H**

BATH

WAY

CRUPPER

ENTERPRISE

BERKSHIRE DR.
PIPERS CT.
BERKSHIRE BUSINESS CENTRE

Colthrop Mill

WAY
MILL LANE
COLTHROP
LANE
MILL LA.
GABLES
COLTHROP LA.

ORD
WAY

Depot

COLTHROP BUSINESS PARK

Colthrop Lock
Colthrop Bri.

11 54
West Berkshire Crematorium
THATCHAM BUS. VILLAGE
COLTHROP WY.
DAYTONA DR.
DR.

Colthrop

Meadowside
Westend Farm
COXS LANE

A4   ROAD

455 17
Nursery Copse
Chester Farm
67
CHURCH ROAD
Carl

Works

Football Grd.

1

Midgham Marsh

Kennet   and   Avon   Canal

ROMAN ROAD (course of)

Midgm Bridge
BRIMPTON

2

66
Qu
Bu
PLY

River
Chamberhouse Mill Cottages
Crookham Manor

Prior's   Moor   Ditch

Aldershot Water

Kennet

Reading

RG7

3

Brimpt Mill

Waterside Copse

Hanging Lands Gully

The Lynch

18

LANE

4

New Gully

Bond's Gully

Earthworks

MANOR

East Field Copse

165

New Gully
Limberlost Farm

White Lodge
POPLAR CL.
JUNIPER PL.
JASMINE WY.
MAGNOLIA CT.
HOLLY CT.
ASH CR.
BEECH
ELM
ROWAN
LARCH DR.
LABURN
FIR CL.
LILAC
CEDAR RD.
LIME CT.
LAUREL RD.
CROOKHAM PARK

Stonehouse Gully

Stone House

Hopgarden Gully

The Plantation

5

Crookh End Hou
Burnell's Farm

ROAD
Hall
Oaklands

Manor Farm

COMMON

MANOR LANE

HYDE

CROOKHAM

RIDDING

Rec. Grd.
Pav.

Little Park House
Little Park Orchard

END

6

Upper Hyde Farm
64

E   **F**   **G**   **H**

Kenton's

Barn Gu
Powell's Copse

25 54
le Park Farm

Hyde End

Marchlands
455
Oa
Cotta

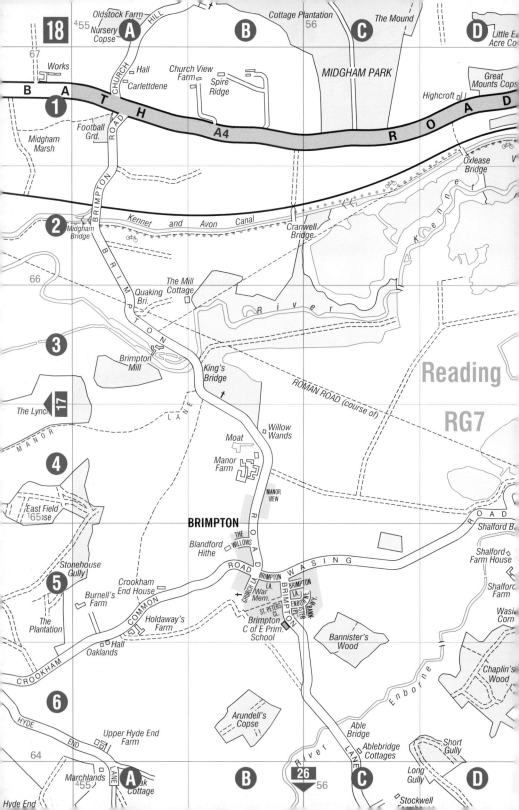

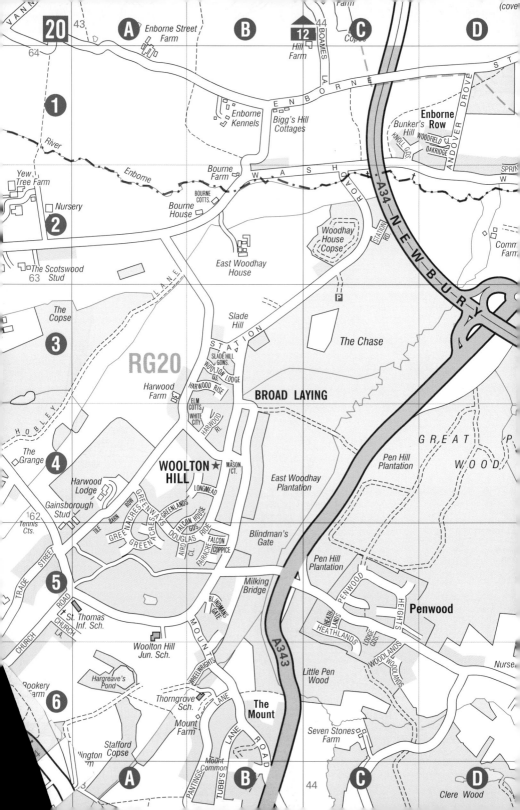

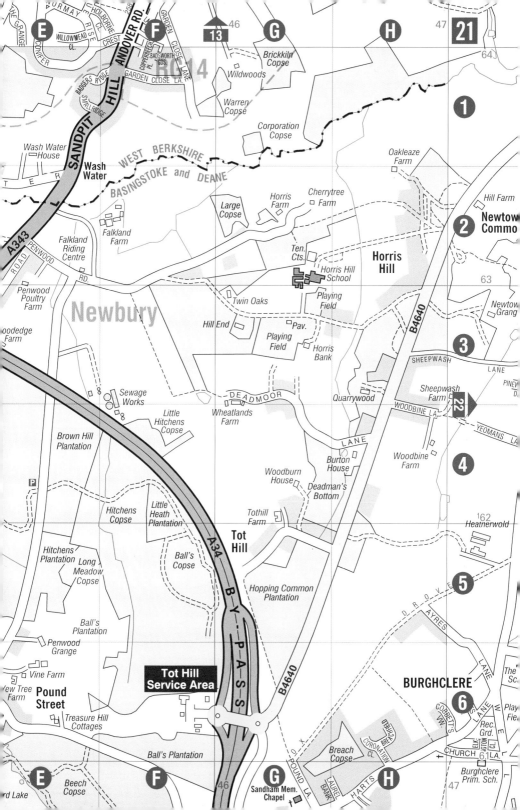

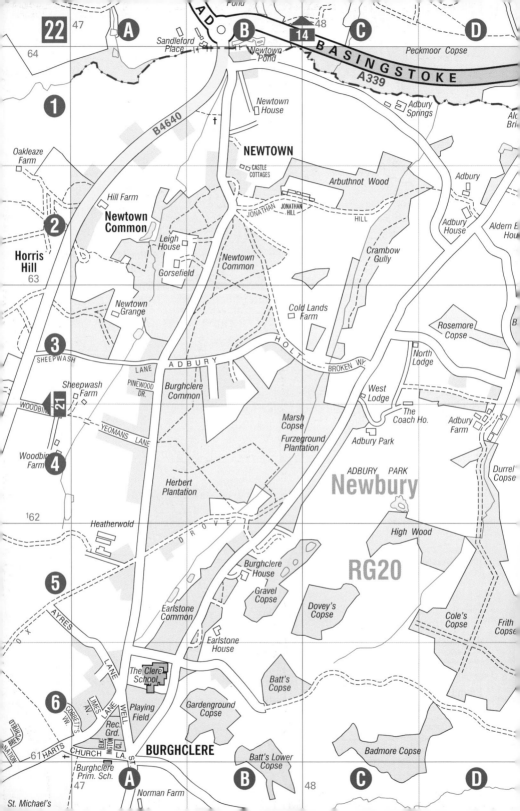

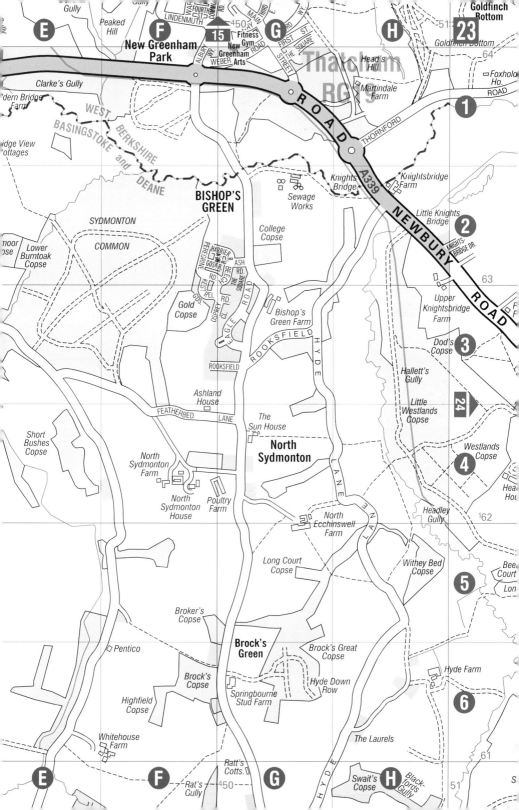

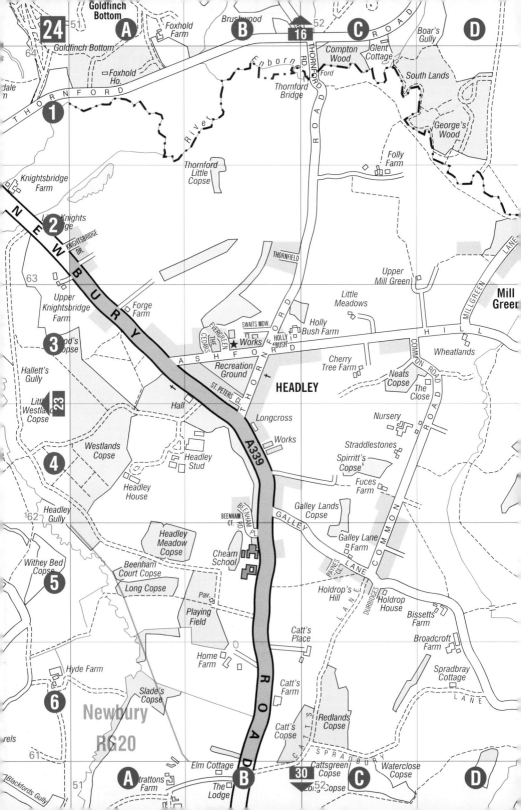

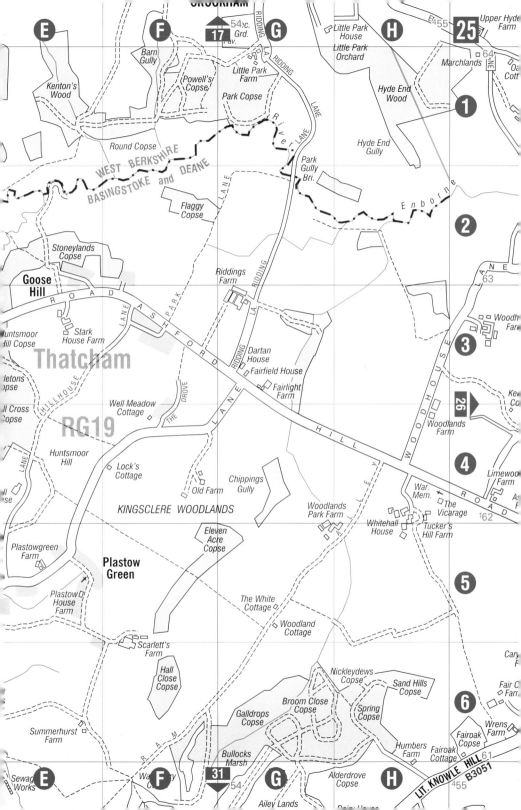

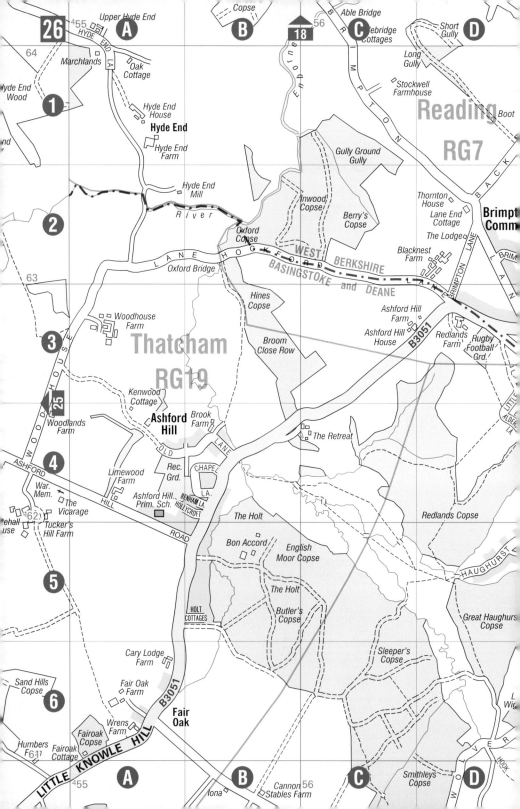

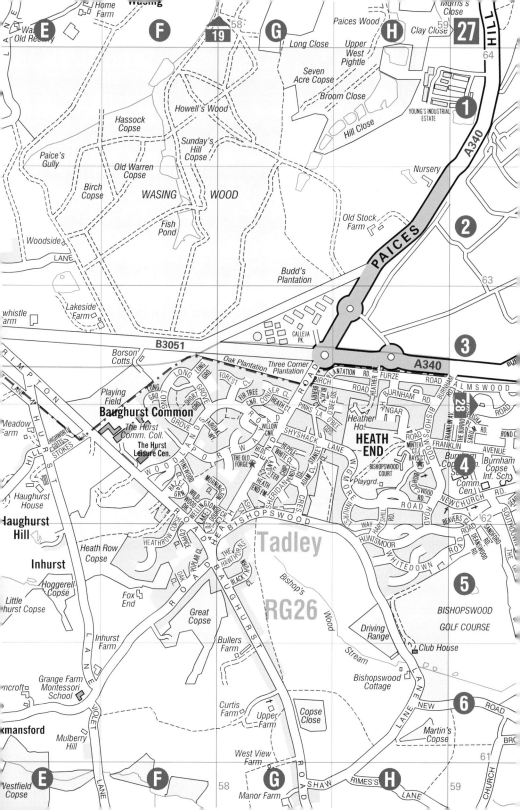

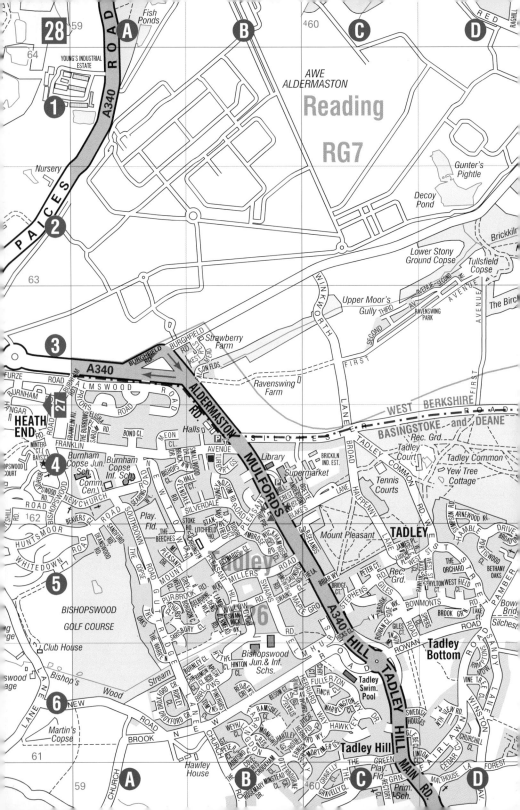

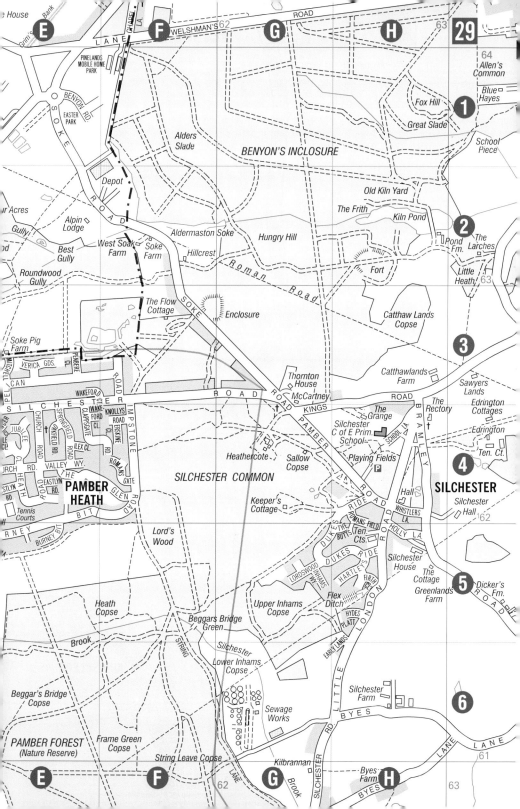

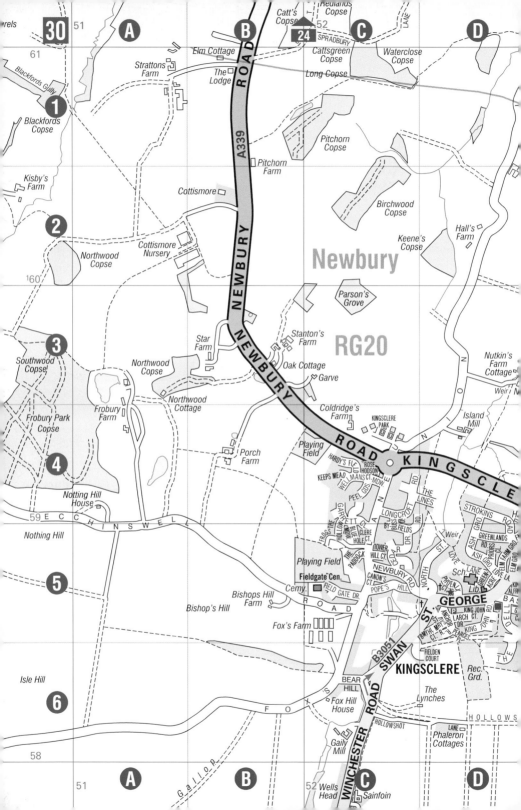

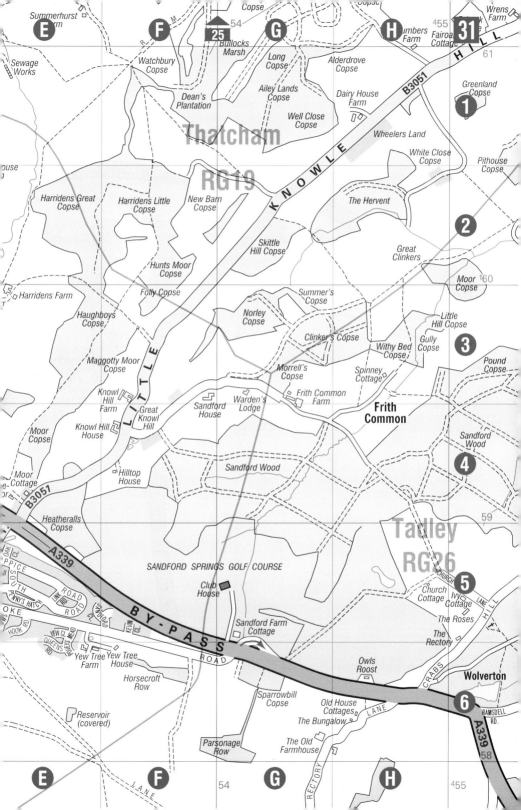

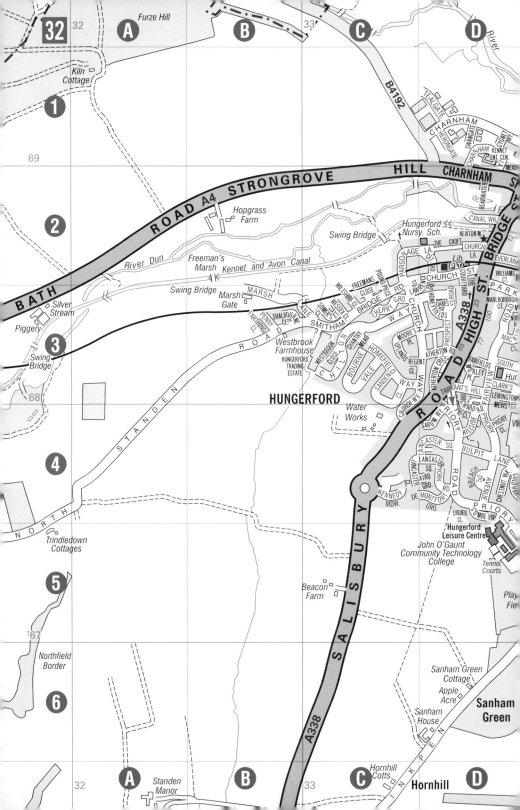

32 32

A   B   33   C   D

Furze Hill

River

Kiln Cottage

1

69

TEAGATE
SWANGATE
CHARNHAM
HERONGATE
CYGNET WY

CHARNHAM
KENNET
ENT. CEN.
MEAD

B4192

2

ROAD A4 STRONGROVE HILL CHARNHAM ST

Hopgrass Farm

Swing Bridge

Hungerford Nursy. Sch.

NEWTON M.

THE CROFT
CHURCH
Lib.
P.H.

BEARWATER

CANAL WK.

NEWTON

River Dun

Freeman's Marsh

Kennet and Avon Canal

PARSONAGE LA.
POUND PIECE
FREEMANS CLOSE
ST LAWRENCE RD
CHURCH
CL.
COURTYARD

EVERLAN
WILLIAMS CT.
PARK
MARLBOROUGH CT.
ROAD
MACK

BATH

Silver Stream

Piggery

Swing Bridge

Swing Bridge

MARSH
LANE
Marsh Gate
SMITHAM

BRIDGE

WILTSHIRE CL.
WESSEX CL.
SOMERSET CL.
SHALBOURNE CL.
PENNY FARTHING CL.

CHERRY GRO.
GRO.
CHURCH ROAD
OAKES CT.
HONEYFIELDS
ATHERTON RD
PROSPECT RD

WAY

HIGH

SOUTH

STANDEN

ROAD

Westbrook Farmhouse

HUNGERFORD TRADING ESTATE

WESTBROOK CLOSE
CHILTON
CHANTRY
UPLANDS
REGENT CL.
MOORE'S PL.

BOURNE MEAD
HOMEFIELD VALE
SANDEN
CL.

ROAD

FAIRFIELDS
APLEY
FAIRVIEW

CLARK'S
LEWINGTON MEWS
Hur

3

68

HUNGERFORD

Water Works

CHURCH WAY

TARRANT'S HILL

SARUM
HILLSIDE
PRIORY
PRIORY

4

NORTH

Trindledown Cottages

LANCASTER SQ.
LANCASTER SQ.
AVRO GRO.
LANCASTER
DE MONTFORT GRO.
KENNEDY MDW.
YORK GRO.

ROAD

BULPIT

BEACH

AVENUE
CHESTNUT WY
COOMBE

LANE

PRIORY

LIGUEIL CL.
COMBE VW.

Hungerford Leisure Centre

John O'Gaunt Community Technology College

Tennis Courts

Play Fie

5

167

Northfield Border

SALISBURY

Beacon Farm

Sanham Green Cottage

Apple Acre

Sanham Green

6

A338

Sanham House

A   B   33   C   Hornhill Cotts.   D

32

Standen Manor

KINTBURY

Hornhill

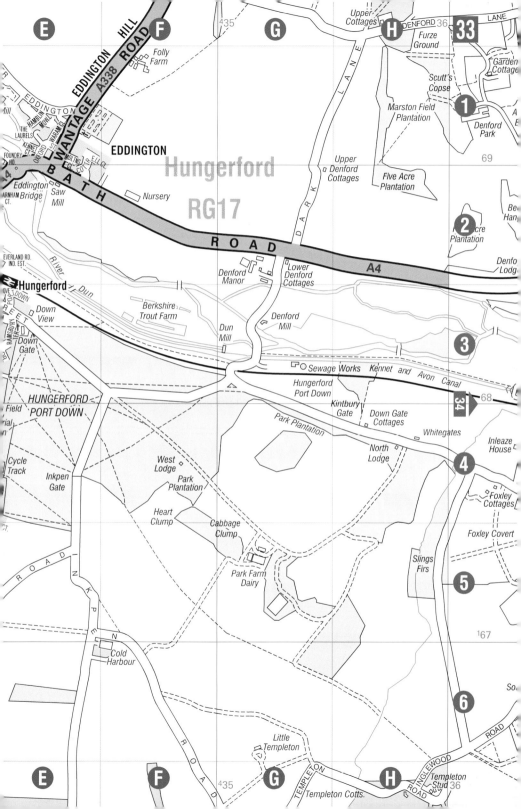

E   **F**   **G**   **H**

EDDINGTON HILL

WANTAGE A338

BATH

435

Folly Farm

EDDINGTON

Upper Cottages

DENFORD 36

LANE

33

Furze Ground

Garden Cottage

Scutt's Copse

Marston Field Plantation

Denford Park

1

69

Hungerford

RG17

THE LAURELS

Mill

HAMBLIN

MOVAL

KENNET

OXFORD

WARHAM

MOLINS

CONTR

ELL CL.

Nursery

Eddington Bridge

Saw Mill

ARNHAM CT.

FOUNDRY HO.

Upper Denford Cottages

Five Acre Plantation

DARK LANE

Acre Plantation

2

Denfo Lodg

EVERLAND RD. IND. EST.

ROAD

A4

Hungerford

River Dun

Down View

Down Gate

Denford Manor

Berkshire Trout Farm

Dun Mill

Lower Denford Cottages

Denford Mill

3

RAMSBURY

OVE

PORT

DOWN

STREET

Sewage Works

Kennet and Avon Canal

68

34

HUNGERFORD PORT DOWN

Field

rial

Cycle Track

Inkpen Gate

West Lodge

Park Plantation

Heart Clump

Park Plantation

Cabbage Clump

Hungerford Port Down

Kintbury Gate

Down Gate Cottages

North Lodge

Whitegates

Inleaze House

4

Foxley Cottages

Foxley Covert

Slings Firs

5

167

Park Farm Dairy

ROAD

INKPEN

CT.

Cold Harbour

6

Little Templeton

TEMPLETON ROAD

INGLEWOOD ROAD

Templeton Stud 36

Templeton Cotts.

E   **F**   **G**   **H**

435

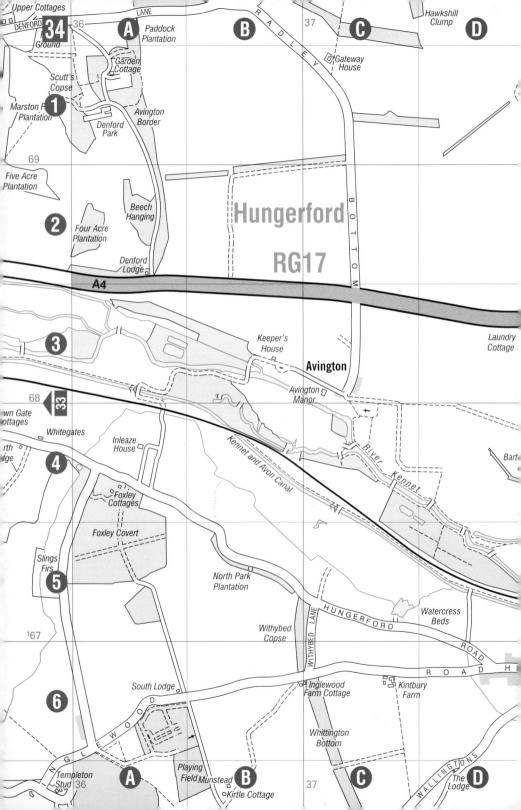

Upper Cottages

DENFORD

LANE

A Paddock Plantation

B

RADLEY

37

C

Hawkshill Clump

D

36

Ground

Garden Cottage

Gateway House

Scutt's Copse

1

Marston P. Plantation

Avington Border

Denford Park

69

Five Acre Plantation

Beech Hanging

2

Four Acre Plantation

Denford Lodge

Hungerford

RG17

BOTTOM

A4

3

Keeper's House

Laundry Cottage

Avington

Avington Manor

68

33

wn Gate ottages

Whitegates

Inleaze House

River Kennet

Bart

rth ge

4

Foxley Cottages

Kennet and Avon Canal

Bar

Foxley Covert

Slings Firs

5

North Park Plantation

Watercress Beds

167

Withybed Copse

WITHYBED LANE

HUNGERFORD

ROAD

ROAD

South Lodge

WOOD

Inglewood Farm Cottage

Kintbury Farm

H

6

Whittington Bottom

NGL

Templeton Stud

36

A

Playing Field Munstead

B

Kirtle Cottage

37

C

WALLINGTONS

D

The Lodge

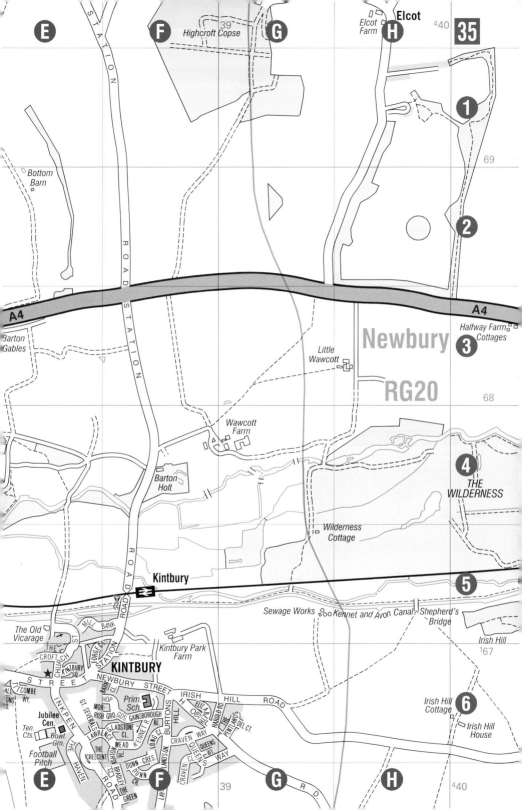

E   F   Highcroft Copse   G   Elcot Farm   H   Elcot   440

1

69

Bottom Barn

2

A4   A4

Barton Gables

Newbury

Halfway Farm Cottages

3

Little Wawcott

RG20   68

Wawcott Farm

Barton Holt

4 THE WILDERNESS

Wilderness Cottage

Kintbury

5

Sewage Works   Kennet and Avon Canal   Shepherd's Bridge

Irish Hill   167

The Old Vicarage

Kintbury Park Farm

KINTBURY

Prim. Sch.

Jubilee Cen.

Ten. Cts.   Bowl. Grn.

Football Pitch

Irish Hill Cottage   **6**

Irish Hill House

E   F   39   G   H   440

INDEX

Including Streets, Places & Areas, Hospitals etc., Industrial Estates,
Selected Flats & Walkways, Service Areas, Stations and Selected Places of Interest.

HOW TO USE THIS INDEX

1. Each street name is followed by its Postcode District, then by its Locality abbreviation(s) and then by its map reference;
e.g. **Agricola Way** RG19: That . . . .1C **16** is in the RG19 Postcode District and the Thatcham Locality and is to be found in square 1C on page **16**.
The page number is shown in bold type.

2. A strict alphabetical order is followed in which Av., Rd., St., etc. (though abbreviated) are read in full and as part of the street name;
e.g. **Hollycroft** appears after **Holly Cl.** but before **Holly La.**

3. Streets and a selection of flats and walkways that cannot be shown on the mapping, appear in the index with the thoroughfare to which they are connected
shown in brackets; e.g. **Anchor Ct.** *RG20: King* . . . .*5D* **30** *(off Anchor Rd.)*

4. Addresses that are in more than one part are referred to as not continuous.

5. Places and areas are shown in the index in BLUE TYPE and the map reference is to the actual map square in which the town centre or area is located and
not to the place name shown on the map; e.g. DONNINGTON 3H 7

6. An example of a selected place of interest is **Donnington Castle** 2G 7

7. An example of a station is **Hungerford Station (Rail)** 2E 33

8. Service Areas are shown in the index in **BOLD CAPITAL TYPE**; e.g. **CHIEVELEY SERVICE AREA** 1C 4

9. An example of a Hospital or selected Healthcare Facility is **THORNFORD PARK BLENHEIM HOSPITAL** 5C 16

GENERAL ABBREVIATIONS

All. : Alley	**Est.** : Estate	**M.** : Mews
App. : Approach	**Fld.** : Field	**Mt.** : Mount
Av. : Avenue	**Flds.** : Fields	**Nth.** : North
Bri. : Bridge	**Gdns.** : Gardens	**Pk.** : Park
Bus. : Business	**Gth.** : Garth	**Pl.** : Place
Cvn. : Caravan	**Ga.** : Gate	**Ri.** : Rise
Cen. : Centre	**Gt.** : Great	**Rd.** : Road
Cl. : Close	**Grn.** : Green	**Sq.** : Square
Comn. : Common	**Gro.** : Grove	**St.** : Street
Cnr. : Corner	**Hgts.** : Heights	**Ter.** : Terrace
Cott. : Cottage	**Ho.** : House	**Trad.** : Trading
Cotts. : Cottages	**Ind.** : Industrial	**Up.** : Upper
Ct. : Court	**Info.** : Information	**Va.** : Vale
Cres. : Crescent	**La.** : Lane	**Vw.** : View
Dr. : Drive	**Lit.** : Little	**Wlk.** : Walk
E. : East	**Lwr.** : Lower	**W.** : West
Ent. : Enterprise	**Mdw.** : Meadow	**Yd.** : Yard

POSTTOWN AND POSTAL LOCALITY ABBREVIATIONS

A'ton : **Aldermaston**	Don : **Donnington**	N Syd : **North Sydmonton**
Ash H : **Ashford Hill**	E Woo : **East Woodhay**	Pad C : **Padworth Common**
Ash G : **Ashmore Green**	Ecc : **Ecchinswell**	Pam H : **Pamber Heath**
Axm : **Axmansford**	Edd : **Eddington**	Pen : **Penwood**
B'nor : **Bagnor**	Enb : **Enborne**	Shaw : **Shaw**
Baug : **Baughurst**	Enb R : **Enborne Row**	Sil : **Silchester**
Been : **Beenham**	G'ham : **Greenham**	Snel C : **Snelsmore Common**
Bis G : **Bishop's Green**	Head : **Headley**	Spe : **Speen**
Brim : **Brimpton**	Herm : **Hermitage**	Stoc : **Stockcross**
Brim C : **Brimpton Common**	High : **Highclere**	Tad : **Tadley**
Buck : **Bucklebury**	H Ben : **Hoe Benham**	That : **Thatcham**
B'clere : **Burghclere**	Hun : **Hungerford**	U Buck : **Upper Bucklebury**
Chie : **Chieveley**	Hun N : **Hungerford Newtown**	U Woo : **Upper Woolhampton**
C Ash : **Cold Ash**	King : **Kingsclere**	W Wat : **Wash Water**
Colt : **Colthrop**	Kint : **Kintbury**	Wint : **Winterbourne**
C Hea : **Crockham Heath**	Mar B : **Marsh Benham**	Wolv : **Wolverton**
Cro : **Crookham**	Mid : **Midgham**	W'peen : **Woodspeen**
Cro C : **Crookham Common**	Newb : **Newbury**	Wool : **Woolhampton**
Cur : **Curridge**	Newt : **Newtown**	W Hil : **Woolton Hill**

A

Abberbury Cl. RG14: Don 3G 7	ALDERMASTON .4H 19
Abbey Cl. RG14: Newb 3A 14	Aldermaston Rd. RG26: Tad 3B 28
Abbots Rd. RG14: Newb 2A 14	Alders, The RG18: That 5B 10
Abbotswood Cl. RG26: Tad 6B 28	Alexander Rd. RG19: That 1C 16
Abex Rd. RG14: Newb 6C 8	Almond Av. RG14: Newb 4A 8
Acorn Dr. RG18: That 3B 10	Almond Dr. RG18: That 5B 10
Adam Ct. RG26: Baug 4G 27	Almswood Rd. RG26: Tad 3A 28
Adbury Holt RG20: Newt 3B 22	Alston M. RG19: That 1A 16
Adey's Cl. RG14: Newb 2B 14	Amberley Cl. RG14: Newb 5H 7
Adwood Ct. RG19: That 6C 10	Ambrose Rd. RG26: Tad 5B 28
Agricola Way RG19: That 1C 16	Ampere Rd. RG14: Newb 6B 8
Aintree Cl. RG14: Newb 2C 14	Anchor Ct. RG20: King 5D 30
Aird Cl. RG20: W Hil 5A 20	*(off Anchor Rd.)*
Albert Rd. RG14: Newb 5A 8	Anchor Rd. RG20: King 5D 30
Albury Way RG19: G'ham 1F 23	Anchor Yd. RG20: King 5D 30
Aldbourne Cl. RG17: Hun 3D 32	*(off Anchor Rd.)*
Alder Cl. RG14: Newb 5D 8	Anderson Gdns. RG26: Tad 4B 28
	Andover Drove RG20: Enb R 1D 20
	Andover Rd. RG14: Newb 1F 21
	RG20: W Wat .3D 20

Angel Ct. RG14: Newb 5H 7	
Angel Mead RG7: Wool 1E 19	
Annadale RG18: C Ash 6H 5	
Anvil Ct. RG18: That 5C 10	
Appleford Cl. RG19: That 1B 16	
Appleshaw Cl. RG26: Tad 6B 28	
Apple Tree Cl. RG14: Newb 4G 13	
Arbour Ho. RG14: Newb 5D 8	
Arcade, The RG14: Newb 6A 8	
Arcade M. RG14: Newb 6A 8	
(off Market Pl.)	
Archangel Way RG18: That 5D 10	
Argyle Rd. RG14: Newb 1H 13	
Arkle Av. RG19: That 6F 9	
Arlington Arts Cen. .4A 4	
Arlington La. RG14: Snel C 4A 4	
Arnewood Av. RG26: Tad 4D 28	
Arnhem Rd. RG14: Newb 6B 8	
Arrowsmith Way RG19: That 1D 16	
Arthur Rd. RG14: Newb 1G 13	

Artillery Dr.—Cavalier Cl.

Artillery Dr. RG19: That 2C 16
Ascot Cl. RG14: Newb 3C 14
Ascott Way RG14: Newb 5D 8
Ashbourne Way RG19: That 6H 9
Ash Ct. RG14: Newb 5A 8
Ash Cres. RG19: Cro C 6E 17
ASHFORD HILL 4B 26
Ashford Hill Rd. RG19: Ash H, Head 3B 24
Ash Ga. RG18: That 5D 10
Ash Gro. RG20: King 5D 30
Ash La. RG26: Baug 4G 27
Ashman Rd. RG19: That 6E 11
ASHMORE GREEN 1H 9
Ashmore Grn. Rd. RG18: Ash G, That 2H 9
Ashridge Ct. RG14: Newb 1A 14
Ash Rd. RG20: Bis G 2G 23
Ash Ter. RG18: Ash G 1H 9
Ashton Pl. RG17: Kint 6F 35
Ashton Rd. *RG14: Newb 1B 14*
(off Kings Rd.)
Ashurst Cl. RG26: Tad 5A 28
Ashwood Dr. RG14: Newb 5D 8
Ashworth Dr. RG19: That 1A 16
Astley Cl. RG14: Newb 1F 13
Atherton Cres. RG17: Hun 3D 32
Atherton Rd. RG17: Hun 3D 32
Atlantean Ct. *RG14: Newb 6B 8*
(off Thornycroft Cl.)
Audley Cl. RG14: Newb 4D 8
Audrey Needham Ho. RG14: Newb 1B 14
Austen Gdns. RG14: Newb 3B 14
AVINGTON 3C 34
Avon Way RG14: Newb 5D 8
AWE Aldermaston 1C 28
AXMANSFORD 6E 27
Aylesford Way RG19: That 1E 17
Ayres La. RG20: B'clere 5H 21
Azalea Rd. RG19: Cro C 5E 17

B

Back La. RG7: A'ton, Brim 5D 18
RG7: Brim 2D 26
Badgers Ridge RG20: Newb 1E 21
Badsworth Gdns. RG14: Newb 1F 21
Bagnols Way RG14: Newb 1G 13
BAGNOR 2E 7
Baily Av. RG18: That 5H 9
Balfour Cres. RG14: Newb 6E 13
Bannister Pl. RG7: Brim 5C 18
Barfield Rd. RG18: That 5G 9
Barley Cl. RG19: That 1D 16
Barlows Rd. RG26: Tad 6B 28
Barn Cl. RG17: Kint 6F 35
Barn Cres. RG14: Newb 4F 13
Bartholomew Cl. RG14: Newb 1H 13
Bartholomew Ct. *RG14: Newb 1H 13*
(off Bartholomew St.)
Bartholomew St. RG14: Newb 1H 13
Bartlemy Cl. RG14: Newb 3G 13
Bartlemy Rd. RG14: Newb 3G 13
Basingstoke Rd. RG7: A'ton 4H 19
RG19: Cro C, G'ham 6B 14
RG20: King 5D 30
RG20: Newt 6B 14
RG26: Wolv 5D 30
Bath Rd. RG7: Been, Mid, Wool 6D 10
RG14: Spe 4B 6
RG17: Edd, Hun 2E 33
RG17: Hun 3A 32
RG18: Colt 6D 10
RG18: That 5G 9
RG19: Colt 6D 10
RG20: Mar B, Stoc 4B 6
Battalion Way RG19: That 2C 16
Battery End RG14: Newb 5F 13
Battle Cl. RG14: Spe 5F 7
Battle Rd. RG14: Newb 5E 13
BAUGHURST COMMON 4F 27
Baughurst Rd. RG26: Baug 5G 27
Baxendales, The RG14: Newb 2C 14
Baydon Rd. RG20: H Ben, Stoc 3A 6
Bayer Ho. RG14: Newb 5H 7
Bays Ct. RG26: Tad 4H 27
Beancroft Rd. RG19: That 1B 16
Bear Hill RG20: King 6C 30
Bear La. RG14: Newb 6A 8
Bearwater RG17: Hun 2D 32
Beavers Cl. RG26: Tad 4A 28
Bedford Cl. RG14: Newb 6E 13
Beech Cl. RG19: Cro C 6E 17
Beech Ct. *RG14: Newb 5A 8*
(off Park End)
Beeches, The RG26: Tad 5A 28
Beech Rd. RG20: Bis G 2G 23
Beech Wlk. RG19: That 1C 16
Beenham Ct. RG19: Head 4B 24
Beenham Pl. Rd. RG19: Head 4B 24
Bell Hill RG14: Enb 6E 13
Bell Holt RG14: Newb 6E 13
BELMONT 3E 7
Belvedere Dr. RG14: Newb 3A 14
Benedict Ct. RG14: Newb 5H 7
Benett Cl. RG14: Newb 4H 7
Benett Gdns. RG14: Newb 4H 7
Benham Chase RG20: Stoc 4A 6
Benham Hill RG18: That 5F 9
Benham La. RG19: Ash H 4B 26
Benyon Rd. RG7: A'ton 1E 29
Berkeley Rd. RG14: Newb 1H 13
Berkshire Bus. Cen. RG19: That 1E 17
Berkshire Dr. RG19: That 1E 17
Bermer Ho. *RG14: Newb 5A 8*
(off London Rd.)
Berrys Rd. RG7: U Buck 3G 11
Besom Ct. RG26: Tad 6B 28
Bethany Oaks RG26: Tad 5D 28
Betteridge Rd. RG19: That 1D 16
Beverley Cl. RG18: That 5A 10
Bewicks Reach RG14: Newb 6H 7
Billington Way RG18: That 3A 10
Birch Av. RG19: Cro C 6F 17
Birch Rd. RG26: Tad 3G 27
Birchwood Rd. RG14: Newb 5D 8
Birds La. RG7: Mid 5H 11
RG18: Herm 2B 4
Bishops Cl. RG26: Tad 4A 28
BISHOP'S GREEN 2G 23
Bishopswood Ct. RG26: Tad 4H 27
Bishopswood La. RG26: Baug, Tad 4G 27
Bishopswood Rd. RG26: Tad 4H 27
Bishopwood Golf Course 6H 27
Blackberry Ct. RG26: Baug 3G 27
Blackdown Way RG19: That 1A 16
Blacklands Rd. RG7: U Buck 4G 11
Blackthorn Cl. RG26: Baug 5G 27
Blackthorn Dr. RG18: That 4B 10
Blagden Cl. RG19: G'ham 3D 14
Blake's La. RG26: Tad 4B 28
Bledlow Cl. RG14: Newb 6F 13
Blenheim Rd. RG14: Newb 1H 13
Blindmans Ga. RG20: W Hil 5B 20
Bluebell Way RG18: That 4B 10
Bluecoats RG18: That 5B 10
Blue Mdw. RG20: King 5C 30
Blyth Av. RG19: That 1C 16
Boames La. RG20: Enb 5B 12
Bodin Gdns. RG14: Newb 3A 14
Bodmin Cl. RG19: That 1A 16
Bolingbroke Way RG19: That 6D 10
Bolton Pl. RG14: Newb 6A 8
Bomford Cl. RG18: Herm 1F 5
Bond Cl. RG26: Tad 4A 28
Bone La. RG14: Newb 6B 8
Bonemill La. RG20: Enb 1F 13
Borderers Gdns. RG19: That 2B 16
Bordon Cl. RG26: Tad 5A 28
Boscawen Way RG19: That 6E 11
Botany Cl. RG19: That 6D 10
Boundary Rd. RG14: Newb 6B 8
Bourne Arch RG18: That 5H 9
Bourne Cotts. RG20: E Woo 2B 20
Bourne Rd. RG19: That 5H 9
Bourne Va. RG17: Hun 3C 32
Bowdown Ct. RG14: Newb 1H 13
Bowdown Woods Nature Reserve 3G 15
Bowes Rd. RG19: That 1B 16
Bowling Grn. Rd. RG18: That 4G 9
Bowmonts Rd. RG26: Tad 5C 28
Boxshall Ct. RG14: Newb 1H 13
Brackenwood Dr. RG26: Tad 4A 28
Bradley Cl. RG17: Kint 6F 35
Bradley-Moore Sq. RG18: That 4C 10
Braemore Cl. RG19: That 2B 16
Brambles, The RG14: Newb 3G 13
Bramdean Cl. RG26: Tad 6B 28
Bramley Rd. RG7: Sil 4H 29
Bramlings Ho. *RG14: Newb 5B 8*
(off Craven Dene)
Bramwell Cl. RG19: That 1D 16
Branch End RG14: Newb 4C 8
Braunfels Wlk. RG14: Newb 1G 13
Breachfield RG20: B'clere 6H 21
Breach Sq. RG17: Hun 4D 32
Brent Cl. RG19: That 1B 16
Briants Piece RG18: Herm 1H 5
Briar Way RG26: Tad 5C 28
Brickiln Ind. Est. RG26: Tad 4C 28
Bridge Ct. RG26: Tad 5C 28
Bridge St. RG14: Newb 6A 8
RG17: Hun 2D 32
Briff La. RG7: Buck, U Buck 3F 11
Brimley Hill Ct. RG20: King 5D 30
BRIMPTON 5B 18
BRIMPTON COMMON 2D 26
Brimpton La. RG7: Brim, Brim C 5B 18
Brimpton Rd. RG7: Brim C 3E 27
RG7: Brim, Mid 2A 18
RG26: Baug 3E 27
Brindley Ct. *RG14: Newb 5H 7*
(off Cherry Cl.)
Broad Halfpenny La. RG26: Tad 4C 28
Broad La. RG7: Buck 1D 10
BROAD LAYING 4B 20
Broadmeadow End RG18: That 5D 10
Broadoak RG26: Tad 5D 28
Broadway RG19: That 6B 10
Broadway, The RG14: Newb 5H 7
Broadway Courtyard RG19: That 6B 10
BROCK'S GREEN 6G 23
Broken Way RG20: Newt 3C 22
Bronte Ri. RG14: Newb 3B 14
Brook Grn. RG26: Tad 5D 28
Brookside Wlk. RG26: Tad 5C 28
Brooks Rd. RG18: That 5C 10
Brookvale Ct. RG14: Newb 5D 8
Brookway RG14: Newb 1E 15
Brookway Trad. Est. RG14: Newb 6E 9
Browning Cl. RG18: That 5A 10
Brownsfield Rd. RG18: That 5A 10
Browns Wlk. RG19: G'ham 4B 14
Bruan Rd. RG14: Newb 3H 13
Brummell Rd. RG14: Newb 5G 7
Brunel Ct. *RG14: Newb 5H 7*
(off Old College Rd.)
RG19: That 6G 9
(off Pound La.)
Buckingham Rd. RG14: Newb 2G 13
Bucklebury La. RG18: C Ash 5H 5
Buckner-Croke Way RG19: G'ham 6F 15
Bulpit La. RG17: Hun 4D 32
Bunkers Hill RG14: Newb 6E 13
Burchell Rd. RG14: Newb 4G 7
Burdwood Cen., The RG19: That 1C 16
BURGHCLERE 6A 22
Burghfield Rd. RG26: Tad 3A 28
Burney Bit RG26: Pam H 5E 29
Burnham Rd. RG26: Tad 3H 27
Burnley Cl. RG26: Tad 6B 28
Burns Wlk. RG18: That 5A 10
Burrows, The RG26: Tad 4A 28
Burtons Hill RG17: Kint 6F 35
BURY'S BANK 4E 15
Bury's Bank Rd. RG19: G'ham 4C 14
Bushnells Dr. RG20: King 5C 30
Butson Cl. RG14: Newb 6G 7
Buttercup Pl. RG18: That 5B 10
Butterfield Ho. *RG14: Newb 1A 14*
(off St John's Rd.)
Butts, The RG7: Sil 5H 29
Byes La. RG7: Sil 6H 29
Byfields Rd. RG20: King 5C 30
Byles Grn. RG7: U Buck 2G 11
Byron Cl. RG14: Newb 4H 13

C

Cairngorm Rd. RG19: That 1B 16
Calard Dr. RG18: That 4G 9
Calleva Pk. RG7: A'ton 3G 27
Canal Vw. Rd. RG14: Newb 6D 8
Canal Wlk. RG14: Newb 6A 8
RG17: Hun 2D 32
Candover Cl. RG26: Tad 6B 28
Canon's Ct. RG20: King 5C 30
Cansfield End RG14: Newb 6H 7
Capability Way RG19: G'ham 4B 14
Carnarvon Pl. RG14: Newb 2H 13
Carnegie Rd. RG14: Newb 1A 14
Carrington Cres. RG26: Tad 5B 28
Cary Cl. RG14: Newb 5F 13
Castle Cotts. RG20: Newt 2B 22
Castle Gro. RG14: Newb 4H 7
Castle Ind. Pk. RG14: Newb 4C 8
Castle La. RG14: Don 3G 7
Castle Way RG14: Newb 4C 8
Catherine Rd. RG14: Newb 1A 14
Catt's La. RG19: Head 6C 24
Caunter Rd. RG14: Spe 5F 7
Cavalier Cl. RG14: Newb 4C 8

Cavalry Cl.—Eliot Cl.

Cavalry Cl. RG19: That . . . 2C **16**
Cavendish Ct. RG14: Newb . . . 4E **9**
Cedar Cl. RG26: Tad . . . 6D **28**
Cedar Dr. RG20: King . . . 5C **30**
Cedar Gro. RG19: That . . . 6A **10**
Cedar Mt. RG14: Newb . . . 3H **13**
Cedar Ri. RG19: Cro C . . . 6F **17**
Cedars, The RG14: Newb . . . 4C **14**
RG19: Head . . . 3B **24**
Celandine Gro. RG18: That . . . 5D **10**
Chalford Rd. RG14: Newb . . . 1G **13**
Chalky La. RG18: Cur . . . 2B **4**
Chamberhouse Mill La. RG19: That . . . 2D **16**
Chandos Rd. RG14: Newb . . . 3H **13**
Chantry Mead RG17: Hun . . . 3C **32**
Chapel Ct. RG17: Hun . . . 2E **33**
RG18: That . . . 5C **10**
Chapel La. RG7: Pad C . . . 1F **29**
RG18: Cur . . . 3E **5**
RG19: Ash H . . . 4B **26**
Chapel Rd. RG20: Stoc . . . 3A **6**
Chapel St. RG18: That . . . 6B **10**
Chapel St. Farmhouse *RG18: That . . . 5B* ***10***
(off Chapel St.)
Chapman Wlk. RG18: That . . . 5H **9**
Charles St. RG14: Newb . . . 5F **13**
Charlock Cl. RG18: That . . . 4C **10**
Charlotte Cl. RG18: Herm . . . 1G **5**
Charlottown RG14: Newb . . . 2C **14**
Charlton Pl. RG14: Newb . . . 5A **8**
Charmwood Cl. RG14: Newb . . . 4H **7**
Charnham Ct. RG17: Hun . . . 2E **33**
Charnham La. RG17: Hun . . . 1D **32**
Charnham Pk. RG17: Hun . . . 1D **32**
Charnham St. RG17: Hun . . . 2D **32**
Charter Rd. RG14: Newb . . . 4H **13**
Chase, The RG14: Don . . . 2H **7**
Chaucer Cres. RG14: Newb . . . 4G **7**
Cheap St. RG14: Newb . . . 1A **14**
Cheriton Cl. RG14: Newb . . . 3B **14**
RG26: Tad . . . 6B **28**
Cherry Cl. RG14: Newb . . . 4H **7**
Cherry Gro. RG17: Hun . . . 3C **32**
Chester Cl. RG14: Newb . . . 3C **14**
Chesterfield Rd. RG14: Newb . . . 2A **14**
Chesterton Rd. RG18: That . . . 4A **10**
Chestnut Ct. *RG14: Newb . . . 5A* ***8***
(off Victoria Gdns.)
Chestnut Cres. RG14: Newb . . . 5A **8**
Chestnut Wlk. RG17: Hun . . . 4D **32**
Cheviot Cl. RG14: Newb . . . 6E **13**
CHIEVELEY SERVICE AREA . . . **1C 4**
Chiltern Cl. RG14: Newb . . . 6E **13**
Chilton Way RG17: Hun . . . 3C **32**
Chippendale Cl. RG26: Baug . . . 4G **27**
Cholsey Rd. RG19: That . . . 6D **10**
Christie Hgts. RG14: Newb . . . 3B **14**
Christopher Ct. RG14: Newb . . . 1B **14**
Christy Ct. RG26: Tad . . . 6C **28**
Church Brook RG26: Tad . . . 6A **28**
Church Cl. RG19: That . . . 6B **10**
RG20: C Hea . . . 5A **12**
Church Ga. RG19: That . . . 6B **10**
Church Hill RG7: Mid . . . 1A **18**
Churchill Cl. RG26: Tad . . . 6D **28**
Church La. RG7: Brim . . . 5B **18**
RG14: Spe . . . 5F **7**
RG17: Hun . . . 2D **32**
RG19: That . . . 6B **10**
RG20: B'clere . . . 6A **22**
RG20: C Hea, Enb . . . 5A **12**
RG20: W Hil . . . 5A **20**
RG26: Wolv . . . 5H **31**
Church Rd. RG7: A'ton . . . 4H **19**
RG14: Shaw . . . 4A **8**
RG20: Stoc . . . 4A **6**
RG20: W Hil . . . 6A **20**
RG26: Pam H . . . 4E **29**
RG26: Tad . . . 6B **28**
Church St. RG17: Hun . . . 2D **32**
RG17: Kint . . . 6E **35**
Church Way RG17: Hun . . . 3C **32**
CITY . . . **2H 13**
Clappsgate Rd. RG26: Pam H . . . 4E **29**
Claremont Cres. RG14: Newb . . . 5D **8**
Clarendon Gdns. RG14: Newb . . . 5A **8**
Clare Wlk. RG14: Newb . . . 5E **13**
Clark's Gdns. RG17: Hun . . . 3D **32**
Clayhill Cres. RG14: Newb . . . 4D **8**
Clere Ct. RG20: King . . . 5C **30**
Clerewater Pl. RG19: That . . . 6F **9**
Cleveland Gro. RG14: Newb . . . 6H **7**
Clifton Rd. RG14: Newb . . . 1G **13**
Close, The RG18: That . . . 5H **9**
Clough Dr. RG18: Herm . . . 1F **5**
Coachmans Ct. RG14: Newb . . . 4B **8**
Cobbett's Vw. RG20: B'clere . . . 6H **21**
Cochrane Cl. RG19: That . . . 6C **10**
Cods Hill RG7: Been, U Woo . . . 1H **19**
COLD ASH . . . **2A 10**
Cold Ash Hill RG18: C Ash, That . . . 6H **5**
Coldharbour Rd. RG17: Hun . . . 4D **32**
Coldstream Way RG19: That . . . 1B **16**
Collaroy Glen RG18: C Ash . . . 1B **10**
Collaroy Rd. RG18: C Ash . . . 2A **10**
Collins Cl. RG14: Newb . . . 5C **8**
Collins Dr. RG18: Herm . . . 1F **5**
COLTHROP . . . **1F 17**
Colthrop Bus. Pk. RG19: Colt . . . 2E **17**
Colthrop La. RG19: Colt . . . 1F **17**
(not continuous)
Colthrop Way RG19: Colt . . . 1F **17**
Combe Vw. RG17: Hun . . . 4D **32**
Common Rd. RG19: Head . . . 3C **24**
Communications Rd. RG19: G'ham . . . 6F **15**
Congreve Cl. RG7: A'ton . . . 4H **19**
Conifer Cl. RG26: Baug . . . 3G **27**
Conifer Crest RG14: Newb . . . 6E **13**
Coniston Cl. RG19: That . . . 6G **9**
Coniston Ct. RG14: Newb . . . 5A **8**
Connaught Gdns. RG19: That . . . 1C **16**
Connaught Rd. RG14: Newb . . . 6B **8**
Connection, The RG14: Shaw . . . 3A **8**
Conway Dr. RG18: That . . . 4H **9**
Coombe Ct. RG19: That . . . 6C **10**
Coombe Sq. RG19: That . . . 6C **10**
Coopers Cres. RG18: That . . . 5A **10**
Cope Hall La. RG14: Enb . . . 4D **12**
Copperbeech Pl. RG14: Newb . . . 1F **21**
Coppice Cl. RG14: Newb . . . 3B **14**
RG26: Baug . . . 5F **27**
Coppice Rd. RG20: King . . . 5E **31**
Copse, The RG26: Tad . . . 5A **28**
Copse Cl. RG7: Buck . . . 1F **11**
Corderoy Cl. RG19: That . . . 1D **16**
Cormorant Wood RG14: Newb . . . 2C **14**
Corner Mead RG18: C Ash . . . 2A **10**
Corn Exchange, The . . . ***6A 8***
(off Market Pl.)
Coronation Cl. RG20: B'clere . . . 6H **21**
Corporation Cotts. RG14: Newb . . . 5H **7**
Coster Cl. RG14: Spe . . . 4F **7**
Cottington Cl. RG20: King . . . 5E **31**
Cottrell Cl. RG17: Edd . . . 2E **33**
Court, The RG18: That . . . 5B **10**
Courtlands Rd. RG14: Newb . . . 2B **14**
Courtyard, The RG14: Newb . . . 5A **8**
RG17: Hun . . . 2D **32**
Coverts, The RG26: Tad . . . 6B **28**
Cowslade RG14: Spe . . . 4F **7**
Cowslip Cres. RG18: That . . . 4B **10**
Coxeter Rd. RG14: Newb . . . 5G **7**
Cox's La. RG7: Mid . . . 1G **17**
Crabs Hill RG26: Wolv . . . 6H **31**
Crabtree Cl. RG18: Herm . . . 1F **5**
Crabtree La. RG18: Cur, Herm . . . 2E **5**
Craven Cl. RG17: Kint . . . 6F **35**
Craven Dene RG14: Newb . . . 5B **8**
Craven Rd. RG14: Newb . . . 1G **13**
Craven Way RG17: Kint . . . 6F **35**
Crawford Pl. RG14: Newb . . . 6H **7**
Crescent, The RG17: Kint . . . 6E **35**
Cresswell Rd. RG14: Newb . . . 5D **8**
Cricketers RG20: Stoc . . . 3A **6**
CROCKHAM HEATH . . . **5A 12**
Crocus Mead RG18: That . . . 5C **10**
Croft, The RG17: Hun . . . 2D **32**
RG17: Kint . . . 6E **35**
Croft La. RG14: Newb . . . 5G **7**
Croft Rd. RG14: Newb . . . 3H **13**
RG17: Hun . . . 2D **32**
Cromwell Pl. RG14: Newb . . . 6A **8**
Cromwell Rd. RG14: Newb . . . 4C **8**
Cromwell Ter. RG14: Spe . . . 4F **7**
CROOKHAM . . . **6G 17**
Crookham Cl. RG26: Tad . . . 6B **28**
CROOKHAM COMMON . . . **5B 16**
Crookham Comn. Rd. RG7: Brim . . . 5D **16**
RG19: Cro C . . . 5D **16**
Crookham Hill RG19: Cro C, That . . . 5C **16**
Crookham Pk. RG19: Cro C . . . 6F **17**
Cropper Cl. RG19: That . . . 6E **11**
Crowfield Dr. RG19: That . . . 6H **9**
Crown Acre Cl. RG19: That . . . 6A **10**
Crown Ct. RG19: That . . . 6A **10**
Crown Mead RG18: That . . . 6A **10**
Crown M. *RG17: Hun . . . 3D* ***32***
(off The Courtyard)
Culver Rd. RG14: Newb . . . 3H **13**
Curlew Cl. RG19: That . . . 6A **10**
Curling Way RG14: Newb . . . 5C **8**
Curnock Ct. RG14: Newb . . . 2G **13**
CURRIDGE . . . **2E 5**
Curridge Grn. RG18: Cur . . . 3E **5**
Curridge Piece RG18: Cur . . . 2F **5**
Curridge Rd. RG18: Cur . . . 4A **4**
Cygnet Cl. RG19: That . . . 6H **9**
Cygnet Way RG17: Hun . . . 1D **32**
Cyril Vokins Rd. RG14: Newb . . . 1E **15**

D

Dalby Cres. RG14: Newb . . . 3B **14**
Danvers Cl. RG19: That . . . 1B **16**
Dark La. RG17: Hun . . . 2G **33**
Dart Cl. RG18: That . . . 4H **9**
Daytona Dr. RG19: Colt . . . 1F **17**
Deadmans La. RG19: G'ham . . . 5B **14**
Deadmoor La. RG20: B'clere, Newt . . . 3G **21**
Deanswood Rd. RG26: Tad . . . 5A **28**
Deanwood Pk. Golf Course . . . **4D 6**
Deccan Gro. RG19: That . . . 1B **16**
Defence Cl. RG19: That . . . 2C **16**
Dell, The RG20: King . . . 6D **30**
De Montfort Gro. RG17: Hun . . . 4C **32**
De Montfort Rd. RG14: Spe . . . 4G **7**
Dene Way RG14: Don . . . 4H **7**
Denford La. RG17: Hun . . . 1H **33**
Denmark Rd. RG14: Newb . . . 1B **14**
Denmead Rd. RG26: Tad . . . 5B **28**
Denton Cl. RG19: That . . . 1A **16**
Derby Rd. RG14: Newb . . . 2H **13**
Derwent Rd. RG19: That . . . 6G **9**
Desborough Cl. RG14: Newb . . . 4E **9**
Dewberry Down RG18: That . . . 5D **10**
Dickens Wlk. RG14: Newb . . . 3A **14**
Dickson Glade RG19: That . . . 1C **16**
Digby Rd. RG14: Newb . . . 5G **7**
Discovery Ct. *RG14: Newb . . . 1A* ***14***
(off Catherine Rd.)
Dittany Gdns. RG18: That . . . 4B **10**
Doctors La. RG18: Herm . . . 1G **5**
Dolman Rd. RG14: Newb . . . 4A **8**
Dolphin Cl. RG7: A'ton . . . 4H **19**
Domoney Cl. RG19: That . . . 6C **10**
DONNINGTON . . . **3H 7**
Donnington Castle . . . **2G 7**
Donnington Elms RG14: Don . . . 3H **7**
Donnington Grove Golf Course . . . **3F 7**
Donnington Lodge RG14: Don . . . 3H **7**
Donnington Sq. RG14: Newb . . . 4H **7**
Donnington Valley Golf Course . . . **6A 4 & 1H 7**
Dormer Cl. RG14: Newb . . . 5G **13**
Dorneywood Way RG14: Newb . . . 5D **8**
Doublet Cl. RG19: That . . . 6G **9**
Douglas Ride RG20: W Hil . . . 5A **20**
Douro Cl. RG26: Baug . . . 4F **27**
Doveton Way RG14: Newb . . . 5B **8**
Dragoons Cl. RG19: That . . . 2B **16**
Draper Cl. RG19: That . . . 1B **16**
Draytons Vw. RG19: G'ham . . . 4C **14**
Drive, The RG14: Newb . . . 3G **13**
Drove, The RG19: Ash H . . . 4F **25**
Drove La. RG18: C Ash . . . 5H **5**
Droxford Cres. RG26: Tad . . . 6A **28**
Druce Way RG19: That . . . 6B **10**
Dryden Cl. RG18: That . . . 4B **10**
Dukes Ride RG7: Sil . . . 5G **29**
Dunn Cres. RG17: Kint . . . 6F **35**
Dunstan Rd. RG18: That . . . 5C **10**
Durbidges RG19: Head . . . 5C **24**
Dyson Cl. RG14: Newb . . . 6G **7**

E

Eagle Rd. RG20: Bis G . . . 3G **23**
Early Lands RG7: Sil . . . 6G **29**
Easter Pk. RG7: Sil . . . 1E **29**
EAST FIELDS . . . **1B 14**
Eastlyn Rd. RG26: Pam H . . . 4E **29**
Ecchinswell Rd. RG20: Ecc, King . . . 4A **30**
EDDINGTON . . . **1E 33**
Eddington Hill RG17: Edd . . . 1E **33**
Edgecombe La. RG14: Newb . . . 4C **8**
Edgehill Cl. RG14: Newb . . . 4E **9**
Edwin Cl. RG19: That . . . 6D **10**
Eeklo Pl. RG14: Newb . . . 2B **14**
Eight Bells RG14: Newb . . . 1H **13**
ELCOT . . . **1H 35**
Eliot Cl. RG18: That . . . 4A **10**

I

J

K

L

Lipscombe Cl.—Oxford Rd.

Lipscombe Cl. RG14: Newb 1G **13**
Lisle Cl. RG14: Newb 4H **7**
Litchfield Ho. RG26: Tad 5B **28**
Lit. Aldershot La. RG26: Baug 4D **26**
Lit. Knowle Hill RG19: Ash H 4F **31**
RG20: King 4F **31**
Little La. RG7: U Buck 3G **11**
Lit. London Rd. RG7: Sil 6H **29**
Livingstone Rd. RG14: Newb 1B **14**
LivingWell Health Club
Newbury 1B 4
Lodge Gdns. RG20: Pen 5C **20**
London Rd. RG14: Newb 5A **8**
RG18: That 6C **10**
(Chapel St.)
RG18: That 5B **8**
(Shaw Rd.)
Longacre RG14: Newb 3F **13**
Longbridge Rd. RG19: That 1D **16**
Long Cl. RG17: Kint 6F **35**
Longcroft Rd. RG19: That 1C **16**
RG20: King 4C **30**
Long Gro. RG7: U Buck 4F **11**
RG26: Baug 3F **27**
LONGLANE **3G 5**
Long La. RG14: Shaw 3C **8**
RG18: C Ash, Herm 3C **8**
Longmead RG20: W Hil 4B **20**
Lordswood RG7: Sil 5G **29**
Loundyes Cl. RG18: That 5H **9**
Love La. RG14: Don, Shaw 3H **7**
RG20: King 5D **30**
(not continuous)
Lwr. Farm Ct. RG14: Newb 2F **15**
Lower Way RG19: That 6E **9**
Lwr. Woodspeen Ct. RG20: W'peen 2C **6**
Ludlow Cl. RG14: Newb 5E **9**
Ludlow Pl. RG26: Tad 5C **28**
Lynton Ct. RG14: Newb 5A **8**
Lyon Cl. RG19: That 1D **16**

M

McKenzie Ct. *RG14: Newb 4H 7*
(off Ormonde Gdns)
Macklin Cl. RG17: Hun 3D **32**
Maderia Pl. RG14: Newb 1A **14**
Magnolia Ct. RG19: Cro C 5F **17**
Magpie Cl. RG19: That 6H **9**
Main Rd. RG26: Tad 6C **28**
Main St. RG19: G'ham 6F **15**
Majendie Cl. RG14: Spe 4F **7**
Malham Rd. RG19: That 6A **10**
Mallard Ct. RG14: Newb 6H **7**
Mallow Gdns. RG18: That 4B **10**
Malthouse Cl. RG19: That 1D **16**
Malthouse La. RG26: Tad 6D **28**
Maltings, The *RG14: Newb 1H 13*
(off Kennet Rd.)
RG19: That 1D **16**
Malvern Ct. RG14: Newb 2H **13**
Mandarin Ct. RG14: Newb 1C **14**
Mandarin Dr. RG14: Newb 2C **14**
Manor La. RG7: Brim 4H **17**
RG14: Newb 4E **9**
RG19: Cro 6G **17**
Manor Pl. RG14: Spe 4F **7**
Manor Rd. RG20: B'nor 2E **7**
Manor Vw. RG7: Brim 4B **18**
Mansell Dr. RG14: Newb 6E **13**
Mansion Ho. St. RG14: Newb 6A **8**
Maple Cres. RG14: Newb 4A **8**
Maple Gro. RG26: Tad 5B **28**
Maplespeen Ct. RG14: Newb 5H **7**
Marchant Cl. RG19: G'ham 4D **14**
Marconi Rd. RG14: Newb 5B **8**
Market Pl. RG14: Newb 6A **8**
Market St. RG14: Newb 1A **14**
Marlborough Ct. RG17: Hun 3D **32**
Marlowes, The RG14: Newb 3H **13**
Marlston Rd. RG18: Herm 1H **5**
Marshalls Ct. RG14: Spe 4F **7**
MARSH BENHAM **5A 6**
Marsh La. RG14: Newb 6A **8**
RG17: Hun 3B **32**
RG18: Cur 2C **4**
Marsh Rd. RG18: That 5C **10**
Marston Dr. RG14: Newb 4D **8**
Martingale Chase RG14: Newb 5C **8**
Martins, The RG19: That 1D **16**
Masefield Rd. RG18: That 5A **10**
Mason Ct. RG20: W Hil 4B **20**
Matthews Cl. RG19: That 6H **9**
Mayfair Dr. RG14: Newb 2G **13**
Maynard Cl. RG18: That 4A **10**
Mayors La. RG14: Newb 1A **14**
Mayow Cl. RG19: That 1D **16**
Meadow Cl. RG19: That 6A **10**
Meadow Rd. RG14: Newb 3H **13**
Meadowsweet Cl. RG18: That 5C **10**
Meadowview RG17: Hun 2D **32**
Medway Cl. RG18: That 4H **9**
Meldrum Cl. RG14: Newb 5E **13**
Meon Cl. RG26: Tad 4A **28**
Merlin Rd. RG20: Bis G 2G **23**
Mersey Way RG18: That 4H **9**
Meyrick Dr. RG14: Newb 6E **13**
Middle Cl. RG14: Newb 4F **13**
RG26: Pam H 4E **29**
Middleton Ct. RG14: Newb 4E **9**
Middletons Cl. RG17: Edd 1E **33**
Midgham Pk. 1C 18
Midgham Station (Rail) **1E 19**
Military Dr. RG19: That 1C **16**
Mill Bank RG17: Kint 5E **35**
Millers Rd. RG26: Tad 5B **28**
MILL GREEN **3D 24**
Millgreen La. RG19: Head 3D **24**
Mill La. RG14: Newb 6B **8**
RG19: Colt 1E **17**
Mill Reef Cl. RG19: That 6F **9**
Millstream Ho. RG14: Newb 6D **8**
Ministry Rd. RG19: G'ham 6G **15**
Minstead Cl. RG26: Tad 6B **28**
Minter Ct. RG26: Tad 4H **27**
Mitchell Cl. RG26: Pam H 3E **29**
Monica Gdns. RG14: Newb 4C **8**
Monk's La. RG14: Newb 4G **13**
Monkswood Cl. RG14: Newb 4F **13**
Monkswood Cres. RG26: Tad 6B **28**
Montacute Dr. RG19: That 1D **16**
Montague Dr. RG19: G'ham 5B **14**
Montague Ter. RG14: Newb 3A **14**
Montgomery Rd. RG14: Newb 3G **13**
Monument Cl. RG14: Newb 4F **13**
Moore's Pl. RG17: Hun 3C **32**
Moor La. RG14: Newb 6F **7**
Moors, The RG19: That 6A **10**
Morley Pl. RG17: Hun 3D **32**
Mornington Cl. RG26: Baug 4F **27**
Morrish Gro. RG17: Kint 6E **35**
Mortimer Gdns. RG26: Tad 6C **28**
Mortons La. RG7: U Buck 3G **11**
MOUNT, THE **6B 20**
Mount, The RG14: Newb 3A **14**
Mountbatten Cl. RG14: Newb 4B **8**
Mount Cl. RG14: Newb 2A **14**
Mt. Pleasant RG26: Tad 5A **28**
Mt. Pleasant Dr. RG26: Tad 5A **28**
Mount Rd. RG18: That 5B **10**
RG20: High 5B **20**
Muddy La. RG19: That 6A **10**
Mulfords Hill RG26: Tad 4B **28**
Munkle Marsh RG19: That 6E **11**
Musket Pl. RG14: Newb 4A **14**

N

Naseby Ri. RG14: Newb 4D **8**
Nature Discovery Centre, The 1A 16
Nevil Ct. RG19: That 1B **16**
Neville Dr. RG19: That 6C **10**
Newbold Rd. RG14: Spe 4F **7**
Newbolt Cl. RG18: That 4A **10**
NEWBURY **1A 14**
Newbury & Crookham Golf Course 4E 15
Newbury Bus. Pk. RG14: Newb 5C **8**
Newbury By-Pass RG14: B'nor, Don, Snel C 5A **4**
RG14: Enb 4C **12**
RG18: Cur 5A **4**
RG20: B'clere, W Wat 2C **20**
RG20: Enb, Spe, Stoc, W'peen 4C **12**
Newbury Golf Course 1E 15
Newbury Leisure Pk. 6F 9
Newbury Racecourse 2C 14
Newbury Racecourse Station (Rail) **1C 14**
Newbury Retail Pk. RG14: Newb 4B **14**
Newbury Rd. RG18: Herm 1G **5**
RG19: Head 2H **23**
RG20: King 5C **30**
(Canon's Ct.)
RG20: King 3B **30**
(Union La.)
Newbury RUFC 5G 13
Newbury Showground 1C 4
Newbury Station (Rail) **1A 14**
Newbury St. RG17: Kint 6F **35**
Newbury Trade Pk. RG14: Newb 1D **14**
Newchurch Rd. RG26: Tad 4A **28**
New Greenham Arts 6F 15
NEW GREENHAM PARK **6F 15**
New Greenham Pk. Leisure Cen. 6G 15
Newport Cl. RG14: Newb 5B **8**
Newport Rd. RG14: Newb 5B **8**
New Rd. RG14: Newb 2C **14**
RG19: G'ham 4D **14**
RG26: Tad 6H **27**
New Rd. Hill RG7: Mid 1E **19**
Newton M. RG17: Hun 2D **32**
Newton's La. RG20: B'nor 2E **7**
NEWTOWN **2B 22**
Newtown RG26: Tad 4A **28**
NEWTOWN COMMON **2A 22**
Newtown Rd. RG14: Newb 1H **13**
RG20: Newt 4A **14**
Nideggen Cl. RG19: That 6B **10**
Nightingales, The RG14: Newb 3B **14**
Night Owls RG19: G'ham 4C **14**
Norlands RG18: That 4A **10**
Normay Ri. RG14: Newb 6E **13**
Northbrook Pl. RG14: Newb 6A **8**
Northbrook St. RG14: Newb 5A **8**
Northcroft La. RG14: Newb 6H **7**
Northcroft Leisure Cen. 6G 7
Northcroft Ter. *RG14: Newb 6H 7*
(off Northcroft La.)
Northern Av. RG14: Don 3A **8**
Northfield Rd. RG18: That 5H **9**
Nth. Standen Rd. RG17: Hun 5A **32**
North St. RG20: King 5D **30**
NORTH SYDMONTON **4G 23**
Northview RG17: Hun 3D **32**
North Vw. Gdns. *RG14: Newb 5B 8*
(off Newport Cl.)
Northview Hgts. RG17: Hun 3D **32**
North Vw. Rd. RG26: Tad 6D **28**
Northway RG14: Newb 1B **14**
RG18: That 4A **10**
Northwood Dr. RG14: Newb 5C **8**
Norton Cl. RG14: Newb 5E **13**
Nuffield Health Club
Newbury 1D 14
Nuyuu Fitness
Newbury 5A 8

O

Oak Cl. RG20: King 5E **31**
RG26: Baug 5F **27**
Oak Dr. RG14: Newb 2H **13**
Oaken Gro. RG14: Newb 3F **13**
Oakes Ct. RG17: Hun 3D **32**
Oakfield Rd. RG26: Pam H 4E **29**
Oaklands RG18: Cur 4C **4**
Oakley Rd. RG14: Newb 5D **8**
Oakridge RG20: Enb R 1D **20**
Oak Ridge Cl. RG14: Newb 3G **13**
Oaks, The RG14: Newb 4A **14**
RG26: Tad 5A **28**
Oaktree Av. RG19: Cro C 6F **17**
Oak Tree Cl. RG26: Tad 4B **28**
Oak Tree Rd. RG19: That 1C **16**
O'Bee Gdns. RG26: Baug 4G **27**
Observer Dr. RG19: That 1C **16**
Oddfellows Rd. RG14: Newb 1H **13**
Odette Gdns. RG26: Tad 4C **28**
Old Bath Rd. RG14: Newb 5G **7**
Old College Rd. RG14: Newb 5H **7**
Old Forge, The RG26: Baug 4G **27**
Old La. RG19: Ash H 4A **26**
Old Newtown Rd. RG14: Newb 2H **13**
Old Nursery, The RG18: Herm 1G **5**
Old Thornford Rd. RG19: Cro C 6B **16**
Orchard, The RG26: Tad 5D **28**
Orchard Cl. RG7: Wool 1E **19**
RG14: Newb 4C **8**
Orchard Ct. RG19: That 6D **10**
Orchardene RG14: Newb 5B **8**
Orchard Pk. Cl. RG17: Hun 3D **32**
Ormonde Gdns. RG14: Newb 4H **7**
Orts Rd. RG14: Newb 1B **14**
Osprey Cl. RG20: Bis G 3F **23**
Otterbourne Cres. RG26: Tad 6B **28**
Overbecks RG14: Newb 5D **8**
Overbridge Sq. RG14: Newb 6E **9**
Owen Rd. RG14: Shaw 3B **8**
Owletts Gro. RG14: Newb 5D **8**
Ox Drove RG20: B'clere 6G **21**
Oxford Rd. RG14: Don, Newb 4H **7**

A-Z Newbury 41

Oxford Sq. RG14: Newb 5H 7
Oxford St. RG14: Newb 5H 7
  RG17: Edd 1E 33

P

Paddison Ct. RG19: That 1C 16
Paddock, The RG14: Newb 1C 14
  RG20: King 5C 30
Paddock Rd. RG14: Newb 2H 13
Paices Hill RG7: A'ton 5H 19
Pamber Forest (Nature Reserve) 6F 29
PAMBER HEATH 4E 29
Pamber Heath Rd. RG26: Pam H 5D 28
Pamber Rd. RG7: Sil 4G 29
Pantings La. RG20: High 6B 20
Parade, The RG26: Tad 4B 28
Park Av. RG18: That 5B 10
Park End RG14: Newb 5A 8
Park La. RG14: Newb 5A 8
  RG18: That 4B 10
  RG19: Head 3F 25
Parkside Rd. RG18: That 4B 10
Park St. RG14: Newb 5A 8
  RG17: Hun 3D 32
Park Ter. RG14: Newb 5A 8
Park Way RG14: Newb 5A 8
  RG17: Hun 4D 32
Parsonage La. RG17: Hun 2C 32
Parsons Cl. RG14: Newb 1G 13
Pavy Cl. RG19: That 1D 16
Paynes Cl. RG19: Head 5C 24
Paynesdown Rd. RG19: That 6H 9
Peachey Dr. RG19: That 1D 16
Pearces Pl. RG20: King 5D 30
Pear Tree La. RG14: Newb 4C 8
Peckmoor Dr. RG19: G'ham 4C 14
Peel Gdns. RG20: King 4C 30
Pegasus Cl. RG19: That 5G 9
Pelham Ho. RG14: Newb 5B 8
               (off Craven Dene)
Pelican La. RG14: Newb 5H 7
Pelican Rd. RG26: Pam H 3E 29
Pellows, The RG20: King 5E 31
Pembroke Rd. RG14: Newb 6H 7
Penbere Cl. RG26: Pam H 3E 29
Penn Rd. RG14: Spe 4F 7
Penny Farthing Cl. RG17: Hun 3B 32
Penny's Hatch RG20: King 5E 31
Penrose Cl. RG14: Newb 4H 7
Pentangle, The RG14: Newb 5A 8
Pentland Pl. RG19: That 1B 16
Pentlands, The RG17: Kint 6G 35
PENWOOD 5C 20
Penwood Hgts. RG20: Pen 5C 20
Penwood Rd. RG20: W Wat 2E 21
Peregrine Rd. RG20: Bis G 2F 23
Phoenix Cir. RG20: King 5D 30
Phoenix Wlk. RG14: Newb 5E 13
            (off Glendale Av.)
Pigeon's Farm Rd. RG19: G'ham 4D 14
Pike St. RG14: Newb 5B 8
Pimpernel Pl. RG18: That 5D 10
Pinchington La. RG14: Newb 4A 14
  RG19: G'ham 4A 14
Pindar Pl. RG14: Newb 4E 9
Pinehurst RG26: Tad 6B 28
Pinelands Mobile Home Pk.
  RG7: A'ton 1E 29
Pine Ridge RG14: Newb 4C 8
Pinewood Cl. RG26: Baug 4F 27
Pinewood Dr. RG20: Newt 3A 22
Pinks La. RG26: Baug 4G 27
Pipers Cl. RG19: That 1E 17
Pipers La. RG19: That 2D 16
Pipers La. Ind. Est. RG19: That 1D 16
Pipers Way RG19: That 1D 16
Pipit Cl. RG19: That 6H 9
Plantation Cl. RG18: Cur 2F 5
Plantation Rd. RG26: Tad 3H 27
PLASTOW GREEN 5F 25
Platt Ct. RG17: Hun 4E 33
Pleasant Hill RG26: Tad 5B 28
Plumpton Rd. RG14: Newb 2C 14
Poffley Pl. RG19: That 6E 11
Pond Cl. RG14: Newb 4F 13
Pope's Hill RG20: King 5C 30
Poplar Cl. RG19: Cro C 5E 17
  RG26: Baug 5F 27
Poplar Pl. RG14: Newb 4A 8
Poppy Dr. RG18: That 5D 10
Porchester Rd. RG14: Newb 2A 14
Porlock Cl. RG19: That 1B 16

Portdown RG17: Hun 3E 33
Porter End RG14: Newb 3B 14
Portiswood Cl. RG26: Pam H 5D 28
Portway RG26: Baug 4F 27
Posting Ho. M. RG14: Newb 5G 7
Pound La. RG14: Spe 5F 7
  RG19: That 6G 9
  RG20: B'clere 6G 21
Pound Piece RG17: Hun 2C 32
POUND STREET 6E 21
Pound St. RG14: Newb 1H 13
Poveys Mead RG20: King 6E 31
Prancing Horse Cl. RG18: That 6C 10
Preston Pl. RG14: Newb 4D 8
Prince Hold Rd. RG19: That 6F 9
Priors Cl. RG20: King 5D 30
Priors Ct. Rd. RG18: Herm 1F 5
Priors Rd. RG26: Tad 3A 28
Priory Av. RG17: Hun 4D 32
Priory Cl. RG17: Hun 4D 32
Priory Pl. RG17: Hun 3D 32
            (off Tarrant's Hill)
  RG19: G'ham 5B 14
Priory Rd. RG14: Newb 2A 14
  RG17: Hun 4D 32
Pritchard Cl. RG19: G'ham 4D 14
Prospect Pl. RG14: Newb 2A 14
Prospect Rd. RG17: Hun 3D 32
Puffers Way RG14: Newb 1G 13
Purbrook Rd. RG26: Tad 5A 28
Pyle Hill RG14: Newb 2B 14

Q

Quantocks, The RG19: That 1B 16
Quarrington Cl. RG19: That 1C 16
Queens Ct. RG14: Newb 2A 14
Queens Rd. RG14: Newb 1B 14
  RG20: King 6E 31
Queens Way RG17: Kint 6F 35

R

Racecourse Rd. RG14: Newb 2B 14
Raceview Bus. Cen. RG14: Newb 1B 14
Rack Marsh (Nature Reserve) 2E 7
Radley Bottom RG17: Hun, Hun N 1B 34
Raghill RG7: A'ton 1D 28
Railside Cotts. RG7: Wool 1H 19
Railway Rd. RG14: Newb 1B 14
Ram All. RG19: Ash H, Head 6F 25
Ramptons Mdw. RG26: Tad 6D 28
Ramsbury Dr. RG17: Hun 3E 33
Ramsbury Ter. RG17: Hun 3E 33
Ramsdell Cl. RG26: Tad 6B 28
Ramsdell Rd. RG26: Wolv 6H 31
Ravenswing Pk. RG7: A'ton 3D 28
Rawlings Cl. RG26: Tad 5D 28
Rays Cl. RG26: Tad 5D 28
Rectory Cl. RG14: Newb 1H 13
  RG26: Tad 6C 28
Rectory La. RG26: Wolv 6G 31
Redfield Ct. RG14: Newb 5D 8
Redfinch M. RG19: That 6C 10
Red La. RG7: A'ton, Pad C 1D 28
Redshank Ct. RG19: That 6G 9
Red Shute Hill RG18: Herm 3G 5
Red Shute Ind. Est. RG18: Herm 2G 5
Red Shute Mill Bus. Cen. RG18: Herm ..3G 5
Reed Wlk. RG14: Newb 5C 8
Regent Cl. RG17: Hun 3C 32
Regents Ct. RG14: Newb 6H 7
Regnum Dr. RG14: Shaw 4B 8
Remembrance Rd. RG14: Newb 1G 13
Rennie Cl. RG14: Newb 5H 7
Reuben's Cres. RG26: Tad 6B 28
Reynards Cl. RG26: Tad 5B 28
Reynolds Ct. RG14: Newb 6A 10
Rhododendron Wlk. RG19: Cro C 5F 17
Richmond Av. RG19: That 6G 9
Ridding La. RG19: Cro, Head 6G 17
Ridge, The RG18: C Ash ......6H 5 & 1A 10
Ridgeway Cl. RG18: Herm 1H 5
Rimes's La. RG26: Baug 6H 27
Rise, The RG18: C Ash 2A 10
Riverdale Cl. RG14: Newb 5C 8
Rivermead Ind. Est. RG19: That 2D 16
River Pk. RG14: Newb 6B 8
River Pk. Ind. Est. RG14: Newb 6B 8
Riverside La. RG14: Newb 4C 8
River Wlk. RG14: Newb 4C 8
Robertsfield RG19: That 6F 9

Robertson Cl. RG14: Newb 3B 14
Robins Cl. RG14: Newb 4H 13
Rockingham Rd. RG14: Newb 1H 13
Roebuts Cl. RG14: Newb 3H 13
Rokeby Cl. RG14: Newb 4A 14
Romans Fld. RG7: Sil 4H 29
Romans Ga. RG26: Pam H 4F 29
Roman Way RG18: That 5G 9
Rookes Way RG14: Newb 5E 9
Rooksfield RG20: Bis G 3F 23
Rookwood RG20: Stoc 3B 6
Rope Wlk. RG19: That 6A 10
Ropley Cl. RG26: Tad 6A 28
Rosebank Cl. RG26: Tad 5B 28
Rosedale Gdns. RG19: That 1A 16
Rose Hodson Ct. RG20: King 4C 30
Rosemary Dr. RG26: Tad 6B 28
Rosemary Gdns. RG18: That 4C 10
Rosemary Ter. RG14: Newb 1G 13
Rosemoor Gdns. RG14: Newb 5B 8
Rosen Ct. RG19: That 6C 10
Rose Ter. RG14: Newb 2H 13
Rosier Cl. RG19: That 1D 16
Rosyth Gdns. RG14: Newb 3D 14
Rotary Way RG19: That 2C 16
Rotherwick Rd. RG26: Tad 6B 28
Round End RG14: Newb 6F 13
ROUNDFIELD 3F 11
Roundfield RG7: U Buck 3F 11
            (not continuous)
Rowan Cl. RG26: Tad 5C 28
Rowan Dr. RG14: Newb 4A 8
Rowan Rd. RG26: Tad 6C 28
Rowlands Copse RG7: Wool 1E 19
Roy Cl. RG18: Herm 1F 5
Rudland Cl. RG19: That 1B 16
Rupert Rd. RG14: Newb 3H 13
Russell Rd. RG14: Newb 1G 13
Rydal Dr. RG19: That 6G 9

S

Saddlers Ct. RG14: Newb 5A 8
            (off Oxford St.)
Sadgrove La. RG7: Buck 1G 11
Saffron Cl. RG14: Newb 6H 7
Sagecroft Rd. RG18: That 4A 10
St David's Rd. RG14: Newb 1A 14
St Donats Pl. RG14: Newb 1A 14
St George's Av. RG14: Newb 1G 13
St Johns Gdns. RG14: Newb 2H 13
          (off Old Newtown Rd.)
St John's Rd. RG14: Newb 2A 14
  RG19: That 6A 10
St Joseph's Ct. RG14: Newb 5B 8
           (off Charlton Pl.)
St Lawrence Sq. RG17: Hun 3C 32
St Leger Cl. RG14: Newb 5G 7
St Marks Cl. RG19: That 6A 10
St Mary's Ct. RG14: Newb 5A 8
          (off St Mary's Rd.)
St Mary's Pl. RG14: Newb 5A 8
          (off London Rd.)
St Mary's Rd. RG14: Newb 5A 8
  RG20: King 5D 30
St Michael's Rd. RG14: Newb 1H 13
St Nicholas Rd. RG14: Newb 1H 13
St Peters Cl. RG7: Brim 5B 18
  RG19: Head 3B 24
  RG26: Tad 6B 28
St Richards Rd. RG14: Newb 4B 8
St Thomas Ct. RG18: That 5C 10
Salcombe Rd. RG14: Newb 2G 13
Salisbury Rd. RG17: Hun 4C 32
Salisbury Row RG17: Hun 3D 32
          (off Salisbury Rd.)
Sanden Cl. RG17: Hun 3C 32
Sandford Cl. RG20: King 5E 31
Sandford Rd. RG26: Tad 5A 28
Sandford Springs Golf Course 5G 31
Sandham Memorial Chapel 6G 21
SANDLEFORD 5B 14
Sandleford La. RG19: G'ham 4B 14
Sandleford Lodge Pk. RG19: G'ham ...5B 14
Sandown Way RG14: Newb 2C 14
Sandpit Hill RG20: Newb 1E 21
Sandy Cl. RG18: Herm 3F 5
Sandy La. RG18: Cur 3F 5
  RG26: Pam H 6D 28
SANHAM GREEN 6D 32
Sargood Cl. RG19: That 1C 16
Sarisbury Cl. RG26: Tad 5A 28
Sarum Rd. RG26: Tad 4A 28

The representation on the maps of a road, track or footpath is no evidence of the existence of a right of way.

The Grid on this map is the National Grid taken from Ordnance Survey® mapping with the permission of the Controller of Her Majesty's Stationery Office.

Copyright of Geographers' A-Z Map Company Ltd.

No reproduction by any method whatsoever of any part of this publication is permitted without the prior consent of the copyright owners.

SAFETY CAMERA INFORMATION

Safety camera locations are publicised by the Safer Roads Partnership which operates them in order to encourage drivers to comply with speed limits at these sites. It is the driver's absolute responsibility to be aware of and to adhere to speed limits at all times.

By showing this safety camera information it is the intention of Geographers' A-Z Map Company Ltd., to encourage safe driving and greater awareness of speed limits and vehicle speed. Data accurate at time of printing.